English for Negotiating

EXPRESS SERIES

Charles Lafond · Sheila Vine · Birgit Welch

OXFORD
UNIVERSITY PRESS

Great Clarendon Street, Oxford OX2 6DP

Oxford University Press is a department of the University of Oxford.
It furthers the University's objective of excellence in research, scholarship,
and education by publishing worldwide in

Oxford New York

Auckland Cape Town Dar es Salaam Hong Kong Karachi
Kuala Lumpur Madrid Melbourne Mexico City Nairobi
New Delhi Shanghai Taipei Toronto

With offices in

Argentina Austria Brazil Chile Czech Republic France Greece
Guatemala Hungary Italy Japan Poland Portugal Singapore
South Korea Switzerland Thailand Turkey Ukraine Vietnam

OXFORD and OXFORD ENGLISH are registered trade marks of
Oxford University Press in the UK and in certain other countries

© Oxford University Press 2010

Adapted from *English for Negotiating* by Charles Lafond, Sheila Vine, and Birgit Welch
© Cornelsen Verlag GmbH & Co. OHG, Berlin 2009

The moral rights of the author have been asserted

Database right Oxford University Press (maker)

First published 2010
2014 2013 2012 2011 2010
10 9 8 7 6 5 4 3 2 1

No unauthorized photocopying

All rights reserved. No part of this publication may be reproduced, stored in a retrieval system, or transmitted, in any form or by any means, without the prior permission in writing of Oxford University Press, or as expressly permitted by law, or under terms agreed with the appropriate reprographics rights organization. Enquiries concerning reproduction outside the scope of the above should be sent to the ELT Rights Department, Oxford University Press, at the address above

You must not circulate this book in any other binding or cover and you must impose this same condition on any acquirer

Any websites referred to in this publication are in the public domain and their addresses are provided by Oxford University Press for information only. Oxford University Press disclaims any responsibility for the content

ISBN: 978 0 19 457951 3

Printed in China
This book is printed on paper from certified and well-managed sources.

ACKNOWLEDGEMENTS

Prepared for OUP by Starfish Design Editorial and Project Management Ltd

The publisher would like to thank the following for their kind permission to reproduce photographs: Alamy Ltd. pp.12 (Executive discussion/© Richard Vdovjak), 27 (Introduction/© PhotoAlto), 30 (Corporate party/© PhotoAlto), 59 (Cinema/© Aardvark). OUP pp.5 (Executives/Sigrid Olsson/PhotoAlto), 10 (Thoughful executive/Photodisc), 13 (Shaking hands/Photodisc), 14 (Female executive/Aluma Images/Radius images), 18 (Canary Wharf, London/Corel), p.20 (Secretary/Stockbyte), p.22 (Business Introduction/ Steve Betts), p.32 (Female executive/Photodisc), 39 (Tense executive/ Stockbyte), 40 (A negotiation/Digital Vision), 42a (female executive/Bill Cannon/Digital Vision), 42b (male exective/George Doyle/Stockbyte), 42c (female executive/© Sigrid Olsson/PhotoAlto), 49 (A negotiation/ PhotoAlto), 50 (Pollution/Photodisc), 52 (A meeting/Photodisc), 57 (French Mayor/Photodisc), 58 (Female executive/Westend61), 58 (male executive/ Stockbyte), 60 (A meeting/Sigrid Olsson/PhotoAlto), 61 (A meeting/ Sigrid Olsson/PhotoAlto), 64 (Contract/Photodisc), 65 (A negotiation/ Stockbyte).

Cover photos courtesy of: Getty Images (hands/The Image Bank/Biggie Productions), (girl at table/Digital Vision/ULTRA.F); OUP (meeting/Photo Alto/Sigrid Olsson).

Illustrations by: Stephen May

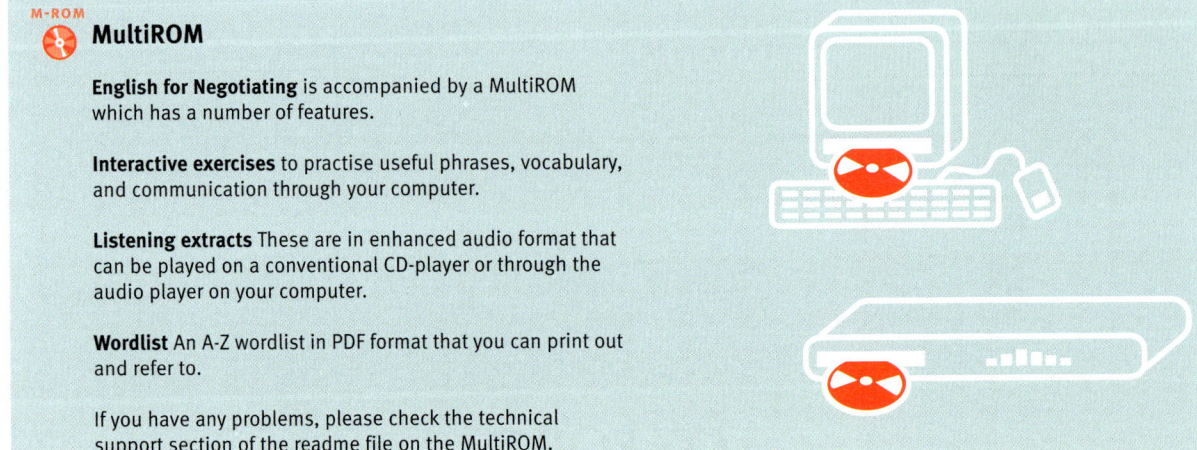

MultiROM

English for Negotiating is accompanied by a MultiROM which has a number of features.

Interactive exercises to practise useful phrases, vocabulary, and communication through your computer.

Listening extracts These are in enhanced audio format that can be played on a conventional CD-player or through the audio player on your computer.

Wordlist An A-Z wordlist in PDF format that you can print out and refer to.

If you have any problems, please check the technical support section of the readme file on the MultiROM.

Contents

PAGE	UNIT	TITLE	TOPICS	USEFUL LANGUAGE AND SKILLS
5	1	Preparation	Setting objectives The HIT table The successful negotiator	Asking for information Planning a meeting Providing explanations
14	2	Setting objectives	Prioritizing objectives Drawing up the agenda Getting to know the other side	Arranging a meeting Stating and asking about interests Agreeing agenda points
22	3	The meeting	Invitation to a meeting Last-minute changes to the agenda The meeting's goals The best approach	Sending a cover letter/email Amending and confirming the agenda Stating goals at a meeting Meeting and greeting
30	4	Proposals	Making a proposal Responding to a proposal Offering a counterproposal	Presenting proposals and counterproposals Clarifying information Expressing possibilities and impossibilities Linking offers to conditions
41	5	A new offer	Types of negotiation Clarifying positions Introducing new ideas Resolving differences	Enquiring about offers Expressing opinions Suggesting a solution
50	6	Dealing with deadlock	Handling conflict Dealing with differences Settling matters	Expressing agreement and disagreement Asking pertinent questions Making and obtaining concessions Encouraging agreement
59	7	Agreement	Finalizing the agreement Setting up an action plan Closing	Describing current and future situations Conveying commitment Stating progress made Setting deadlines Summarizing

PAGE	APPENDIX
68	Test yourself!
70	Partner files Partner A
72	Partner files Partner B
74	Answer key
80	Transcripts
87	Useful phrases

About the book

English for Negotiating is aimed at people who regularly need to negotiate in English at work. This book provides all the language needed to handle the typical scenarios encountered on the way to successful negotiations.

English for Negotiating consists of seven units, covering all the typical stages of a negotiation. Every unit concentrates on one fundamental aspect. At the outset, it is important to prepare thoroughly (Unit 1). After the initial goals have been determined (Unit 2), the first round of negotiations can be organized (Unit 3). Detailed offers are discussed (Unit 4) and counter-offers are presented (Unit 5). Differences are resolved (Unit 6), and finally a successful conclusion can be reached (Unit 7). The units are presented in a logical structure, but can be worked through in any order.

Every unit begins with a **Starter**, introducing the themes and vocabulary of the unit. Listening is a core component of every unit, as are reading texts, which present typical negotiating terms in context. Numerous practice exercises, both spoken and written, offer the opportunity to put what has been learned to use. The **Useful phrases** boxes advise on commonly used idioms. Every unit also contains a **Negotiating skills** box with tips on employing effective strategies and techniques. The **Intercultural skills** boxes give advice on creating a good impression, avoiding problems, and closing the deal, when working with foreign partners. At the end of every unit there is an **Output** text, an authentic text on themes such as best practice, which encourages reflection and discussion.

At the end of the book, there is a **Test yourself!** crossword on pages 68–69. In the appendix the **Answer key** is provided for independent study, along with the **Partner files**, the **Transcripts** of the **Listening extracts**, and several **Useful phrases** boxes.

The **MultiROM** contains all the **Listening extracts** from the book. These can be played through the audio player on a computer, or through a conventional CD player, or can be downloaded onto an MP3 player for extra listening practice. The **Interactive exercises** provide **Useful phrases**, **Vocabulary**, and **Communication** practice, and are particularly valuable for independent study. There is also an **A–Z Wordlist** with all the key words that appear in **English for Negotiating**. This includes a column of phonetics and a space for you to write the translations of the words in your own language.

1 Preparation

STARTER Read the following quotes.

- In business, you don't get what you deserve, you get what you negotiate. (Chester L. Karass)
- The fellow who says he'll meet you halfway usually thinks he's standing on the dividing line. (Orlando A. Battista)
- Let us never negotiate out of fear. But let us never fear to negotiate. (J.F. Kennedy)
- To be successful, you have to relate to people ... (George Ross)
- Failing to plan is planning to fail. (Anonymous)

- Do you agree with these quotes? Explain why. Give examples from your own experience.
- Which of the quotes best fits the unit title? Why?
- Why do we negotiate? Can you think of three reasons?

1 Read the internal email below.

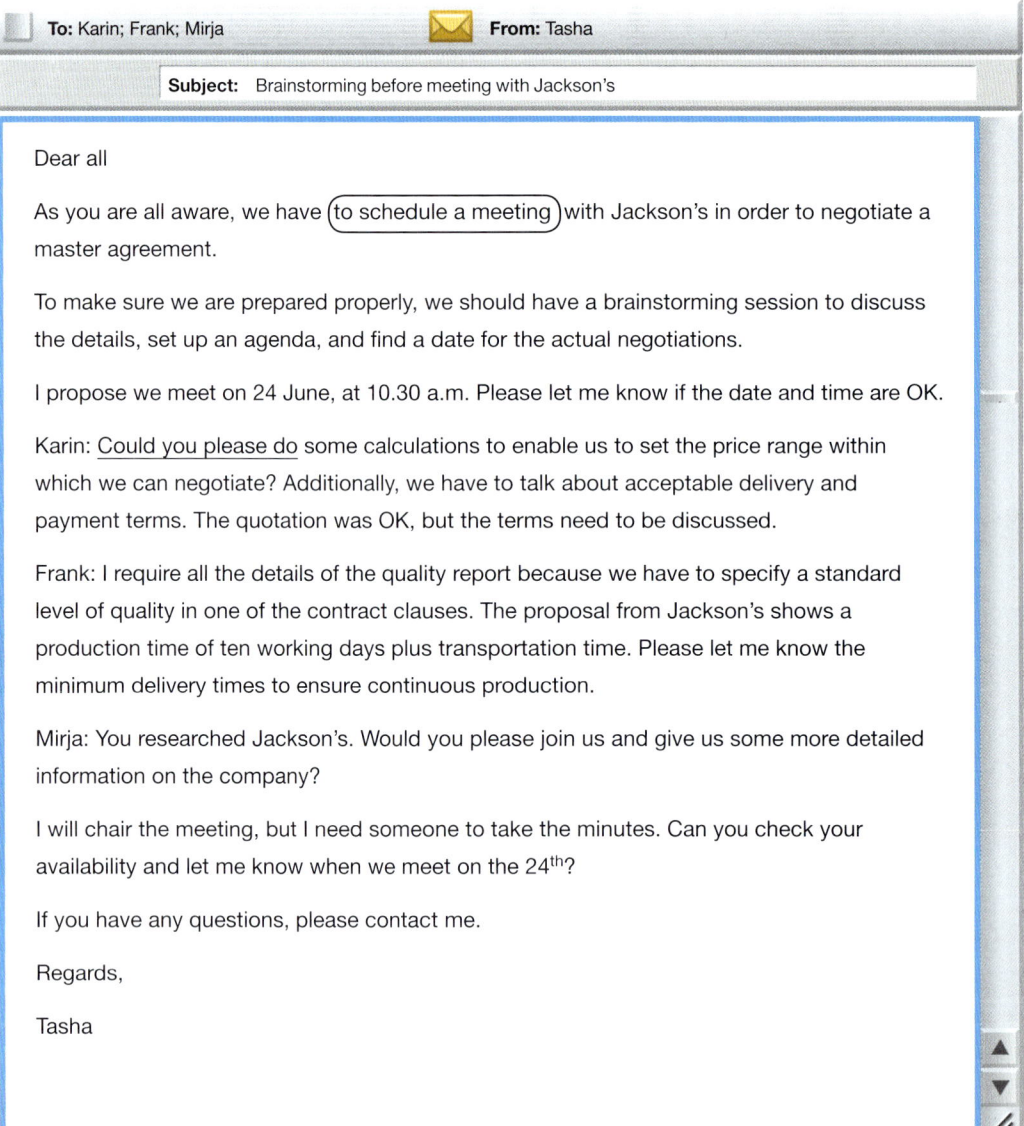

To: Karin; Frank; Mirja   **From:** Tasha

Subject: Brainstorming before meeting with Jackson's

Dear all

As you are all aware, we have to schedule a meeting with Jackson's in order to negotiate a master agreement.

To make sure we are prepared properly, we should have a brainstorming session to discuss the details, set up an agenda, and find a date for the actual negotiations.

I propose we meet on 24 June, at 10.30 a.m. Please let me know if the date and time are OK.

Karin: Could you please do some calculations to enable us to set the price range within which we can negotiate? Additionally, we have to talk about acceptable delivery and payment terms. The quotation was OK, but the terms need to be discussed.

Frank: I require all the details of the quality report because we have to specify a standard level of quality in one of the contract clauses. The proposal from Jackson's shows a production time of ten working days plus transportation time. Please let me know the minimum delivery times to ensure continuous production.

Mirja: You researched Jackson's. Would you please join us and give us some more detailed information on the company?

I will chair the meeting, but I need someone to take the minutes. Can you check your availability and let me know when we meet on the 24th?

If you have any questions, please contact me.

Regards,

Tasha

Now answer the following questions.

1. When does Tasha want to meet her team?
2. Who should be at the brainstorming meeting?
3. Why are they meeting with Jackson's?
4. What should Frank bring to the meeting?
5. How long does it take to make the product?

2 Underline the expressions used in the email to *ask for information*. Put a circle around the ones used to *plan a meeting*. One of each has been done for you.

> **GETTING INFORMATION AND ASKING FOR HELP**
>
> When asking for information or help, you can express your request in either an informal or a formal way. Here are some examples for both.
>
> | **Informal** | **Formal** |
> |---|---|
> | I need … | I would like … |
> | How about … ? | Please let me know … |
> | Where is/are … ? | Do you have any details on … ? |
> | Do you know … ? | What is/are the alternative(s) here? |
> | How is … going? | Who is responsible for/in charge of … ? |
> | Have you got a moment? | Can I ask you a favour? |
> | | Can you help me with … , please? |

3 Certain words have verb and noun forms. Complete the table using words from the email. Compare your results with a partner.

Verb	Noun
to negotiate	1
to propose	2
3	arrangement
to discuss	4
5	preparation
6	calculation
to deliver	7
8	payment

Verb	Noun
to quote	9
10	specification
to produce	11
to transport	12
to chair	13
14	information
15	production
to meet	16

> **WHAT IS NEGOTIATING?**
>
> Trading through negotiation is the basis of human civilization. Negotiation takes place when two or more people have different views and want different things. They come together to try and reach agreement. The negotiator says, in effect:
>
> *'If you give me some of what I want, then I will give you some of what you want.'*
>
> We all negotiate for things each day. We arrange an appointment, ask for better service, ask for a higher salary, or solve an argument with a co-worker or family member.

4 You are working on a project with some colleagues. One colleague needs the following information and some help with tasks. Ask a partner for assistance. Use the information below.

Example: Could you please send me Westworld's address?

Ask somebody for Westworld's address

Ask somebody for the name of a person from the production department

Ask somebody if they are busy

Ask somebody for the address of a delivery company

Ask somebody for an explanation for the word 'haggling'

Ask somebody to finish a calculation

Ask somebody for help on a proposal

Ask somebody to get some information on prices for you

Ask somebody for the yellow folder with the samples

Ask somebody for more information about the material required (i.e. size, colour, thickness)

> **GETTING INFORMATION**
>
> Getting information from business partners is always important. This can sometimes be more difficult when negotiating with people from other cultures. For this reason, it is necessary to try and keep cultural differences in mind.
>
> Do you know these groups?
>
> Group 1: Those who do one thing at a time. They plan each step of their negotiations, meetings, and discussions, and are excellent at organizing their thoughts.
> Group 2: Those who do many things at the same time. They are very flexible and prefer to adapt to the situation. Schedules and agendas mean little to them.
> Group 3: Those who listen quietly and calmly because respect is key. These cultures react carefully to other's proposals. They listen first, establish the other's position, and then formulate their own.
>
> However, don't make quick generalizations about other cultures, and avoid cultural stereotypes! Your business partners will appreciate it.

What experience have you had negotiating with people from other cultures? Do you recognize any of the groups above?

5 **Tasha has asked Karin to come to her office. She needs some information before the meeting. Listen to the dialogue, then say whether these statements are true (✔) or false (✗).**

1 The internal meeting date is on June 22nd.

2 Tasha asks Frank to take the minutes of the meeting.

3 Tasha is not happy with the price Jackson's has proposed.

4 The delivery and payment terms are very good.

5 Karin has lost the quotation.

6 Tasha's objective is to agree a target price.

7 Tasha wants payment terms which are similar to those offered by other firms.

Now listen again and check your answers. Then correct the false sentences.

> **NEGOTIATING SKILLS**
>
> **HIT** refers, in negotiation terms, to **H** – HAVE TO HAVE, **I** – INTEND, **T** – TRADABLE.
>
> A **HAVE TO HAVE** is an essential aspect or outcome for one of the parties in the negotiation. Generally, there are only one or two in each negotiation. However, they are a must! You must achieve these items in order for your negotiation to be successful.
>
> **INTEND** refers to something that is less essential, but still important in the negotiation. You might be prepared to be flexible with respect to these items. You only have a few of them, i.e. perhaps two to five.
>
> A **TRADABLE** item is something you put in your proposal which you believe your partner would like to have. You are prepared to exchange this item for something which you would like to obtain.
>
> Before you begin the negotiations with your partner, it is very important to determine these issues and decide which category they belong to from your point of view. These issues should be clear to all members of your negotiating team. The clearer you are about your goals and needs and those of the opposite party, the more effective you can be as a negotiator. As a result, you are more likely to obtain the result you want.

6 Look at Tasha's options and decide which of the 'H's' she could possibly decide upon. Can you explain why she would choose them?

good payment terms good relationship

good delivery terms discount on large quantities

the right price for the goods **H** presents at Christmas

a wide variety of colours flexibility product quality

nice people to talk to short delivery time

SET SMART OBJECTIVES

When you decide on your 'H's', it is best to set very clear and targeted objectives. To help you define them effectively, it is recommended to set SMART goals.

Your objectives must be:

Specific – state exactly what you want to achieve
Measurable – know how much you have achieved
Achievable – choose realistic goals for the given circumstances
Relevant – find interesting points for both parties
Timed – set a realistic deadline

---

7 Your company must increase production. It needs to move to a new location where new production halls and offices can be built. Work with a partner. Prepare a list of possible 'H's' for your company. Compare your list with a partner and explain your choice. Use the expressions from the Useful Phrases box on page 11.

H

_____
_____
_____
_____
_____

Keep your list of 'H's, because you will need it later.

UNIT 1　Preparation　|　11

PROVIDING REASONS AND EXPLANATIONS	
This is because … .	We need/require … .
The reason for … is … .	We want … .
… is essential for our customers.	We would like … .
These are the most important points … .	This is a must!
We must have … .	The price must fit our guidelines.
We have to have … .	Money is all important!

8 It's June 24th, 10.30 a.m. Tasha is meeting with her colleagues. They all want to hear Mirja's presentation on the potential partner. Listen to the meeting and take notes. Compare your notes with a partner.

Now use your notes to complete Mirja's formal report for the company.

Title: Report on Jackson's PLC

Introduction: This report aims to provide details on the above company so that future business can be discussed.

Findings – The company was founded in _____ [1]. The Chief Executive Officer is Peter J_____ [2], Eng.D., the _____ [3] of the founder. The whole company is based around the Research and _____ [4] division.

Recent developments – They have appointed a new director of _____ [5]. His name is _____ [6] H_____ [7]. He wishes to expand the company into a new area, which is _____ [8]. Most of the current production is sold in _____ [9].

Finance – Their latest accounts show a _____ [10] in profit which has been caused by _____ [11] orders. This means that they have had to _____ [12] their workforce, which could mean that they have lost _____ [13]. Mr Hallam has recently returned from a Chamber of Commerce sponsored visit to China and stated _____ [14].

Proposal – We suggest …

Conclusion – This company could be interesting for us because …

Which additional information would you need if you were Tasha? Make a proposal and justify your suggestions to a partner.

9 Imagine you are Tasha. You now have to make a decision. Use all the information you have gathered to make a decision. Put your reasons under 'For' or 'Against' in the table below.

For	Against

Would you want to negotiate with this company and build a new partnership?

10 You are thinking about expanding your production capabilities. If you do so, you will need a lot more space for your production halls and offices. You and your partner have received different information. Get the information from each other and set your 'H's' in preparation for a negotiation. Give an explanation for your 'H's'.

PARTNER FILES Partner A   File 1, p. 70
              Partner B   File 1, p. 72

Read the article about good negotiating practice.

Excerpt from **Chris James**,
Negotiation Coach for Executives in New York

The successful negotiator

When negotiating, it's extremely important to understand how communication works. According to communication theorist Paul Watzlawick, for communication to take place, you have to have someone to send the message – a *sender* – and someone who receives the message – a *receiver*.

In short, there are two basic laws:

1 It's not what the *sender* says, but what the *receiver* understands that is true.
2 The *sender* is responsible for what the *receiver* understands.

As a result, two truths follow.

1 'One cannot not communicate.' We are always communicating. Even if we stop speaking and say nothing, we would still be communicating something. Most people would probably interpret this as disinterest or perhaps dislike. Normally we ask them, 'What is wrong?'

2 'Communication takes place at two levels: the content level and the relationship level.' The content level is *what* is said – the facts & figures. The relationship level is *how* it's said – the feelings and the atmosphere. It's like an iceberg. 80–90 % of communication takes place under water – at the relationship level.

So if you want to be a successful negotiator, get to know the other side well. Only after that, start planning your offer.

OVER TO YOU

- Can you think of a situation where you do not communicate? Discuss this with a partner.
- Do you agree that most communication is based on relationship and much less on content?
- What makes you a good negotiator?

Setting objectives

STARTER Choose one of the situations below. Brainstorm with a partner a list of points that both partners might want to include in a negotiation. The questions below will help you.

Situation 1
Employees and employer:
the company finds itself in economic difficulty and ten employees have already lost their jobs. The employees are unhappy with employment and salary issues.

Situation 2
Two companies:
one company (an important customer) owes the other company €20,000 but cannot pay it now.

- Why should each party negotiate?
- What does each side want to achieve?

- What are each side's alternatives?
- What is their next best solution?

Afterwards discuss your list with another student who has the same scenario. Then read your list to the class and explain the reasons for your choices.

1 Read the following note.

> Oracle Bank, Latvia and Dominions Bank, Britain, have agreed to merge. However, many details still need to be formalized. The banks are arranging to meet and finalize arrangements. Both parties are currently working on the agenda for the meeting.

What issues might be important in such a merger?

THE AGENDA – THE KEY TO SUCCESS

Any good business meeting has an agenda. Any good negotiation has an agenda, too. Organizing and planning an agenda helps you in three ways:
1. You identify your own issues, priorities, and goals.
2. You identify your opponent's issues, priorities, and goals.
3. It helps you maintain discipline.

'*When you know where you are and where you want to go, it's a lot easier to make the trip.*'

2 Read the following memo.

From: D. DaVita (CEO)
To: H. Gosling (CFO) & J. DaVita (Public Relations Consultant)
Date: 18 January 2010 (CFO)
Subject: Merger meeting – Urgent

ORACLE Bank

Harold, I need you and Johannes to discuss this merger meeting. We do not have to accept all their ideas. But I am quite happy if they choose the venue and appoint the chairperson. I hope 18 February is a suitable date for all.

We must appoint Johannes as our public relations expert. With all the bad publicity that banks are getting following the credit crunch, we are going to need someone to make us look good in the press.

Concerning the corporate centres, I think we will have to agree to close ours. London is a much bigger financial centre. In addition, we can get a good price for the old building. Perhaps we could locate the marketing department in Latvia.

Johannes and I feel that we need to notify customers well before the merger, as many Latvian employees will lose their jobs. We cannot risk a negative effect on the share price as the merger goes ahead.

Now, for the advertising, I am willing to accept the use of a British expert. However, I will agree only if they agree to reduce the number of Oracle branches that have to close in Britain. Our intention is to keep at least a few open.

By the way, my son is interested in combining and updating the computer systems. Perhaps we could trade this idea against the new corporate image. It will look very British anyway due to the British advertising agency. I would also like to add our name to Dominions'. It would be good corporate branding.

I refuse to accept any redundancies among the marketing staff. I will not compromise on this. Some of our people have been with us for 20 years. It may mean that our call centres and some computer centres will have to close. However, these people should soon get new jobs, as there is a need for good people in IT.

Harold, please let me have your thoughts and a proposed agenda by the morning.

DD

Did you mention any of the issues which Mrs DaVita finds important?

16 | UNIT 2 Setting objectives

3 Are the following statements true (✓) or false (✗)? Correct the false sentences.

1. Mrs DaVita wants to be the chairperson at the meeting.
2. She wants the meeting to be in the summer.
3. It is important for her to have Johannes at the meeting.
4. She thinks the headquarters should be in Latvia.
5. She is happy to accept a British advertising company.
6. It is OK with her if all the British branches are closed down.
7. Closing the call centres is not a problem for her.

4 Harold has started to write Oracle Bank's proposed agenda. Help Harold by filling in the missing words. You will find some words to help you in the memo in exercise 2.

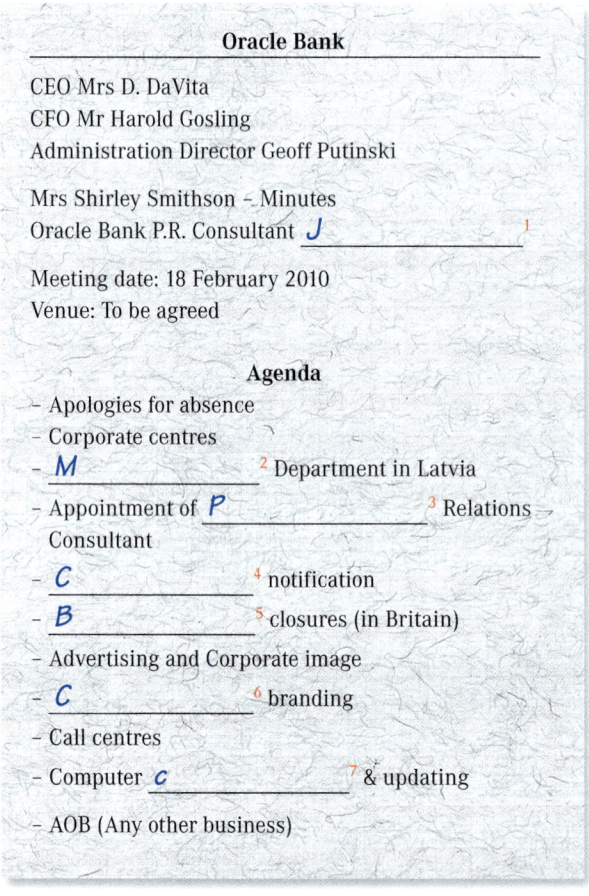

Oracle Bank

CEO Mrs D. DaVita
CFO Mr Harold Gosling
Administration Director Geoff Putinski

Mrs Shirley Smithson – Minutes
Oracle Bank P.R. Consultant J_____¹

Meeting date: 18 February 2010
Venue: To be agreed

Agenda
- Apologies for absence
- Corporate centres
- M_____² Department in Latvia
- Appointment of P_____³ Relations Consultant
- C_____⁴ notification
- B_____⁵ closures (in Britain)
- Advertising and Corporate image
- C_____⁶ branding
- Call centres
- Computer c_____⁷ & updating
- AOB (Any other business)

A Have (H) is something that is an essential.

An Intend (I) is something that is less essential, but still important.

A Tradable (T) item is something you are willing to move on.

USEFUL PHRASES – EXPRESSING HIT		
Have	**Intend**	**Tradable**
We must …	Our intention is …	I am willing to accept … if …
Our main concern is …	I would like to …	I think we will have to agree to …
It is vital/crucial that …	We might like to …	It would be an alternative to …
I refuse to accept …		We can trade this against …
		A few things we can compromise on are …

UNIT **2** Setting objectives | **17**

5 Reread the memo on page 15.
  a Which of the HIT phrases from the box can you find in the memo? Underline them.
  b Decide which are the essential points for Mrs DaVita (H), which are the important points (I) and which points is she prepared to exchange for another point (T), and label them H, I, or T. Now put them into the table. Two have been done for you.

Essential (H)	Important (I)	Exchangeable points (T)
Public Relations Consultant		
	Keep name	

ISSUES, POSITIONS, AND INTERESTS

It's very important to understand the difference between these three points. Clarify them before you finalize your agenda! This will help your preparation become effective.

Issues: The points that actually go on the agenda – what is to be negotiated.
Positions: Your position is what you say you want – what you want to ask for.
Interests: Your interest answers the question 'Why?' – why you want what you want.

It's essential to analyse these points from your side as well as from the opponent's side.

6 Mrs DaVita has not yet received the agenda. Listen to Harold discuss this matter with her. Mrs DaVita changes the order. Help Harold put the points in the order she wants.

AGENDA
1 Apologies for absence
2
3
4
5
6
7
8
9
10
11
12 Date of next meeting

UNIT 2 Setting objectives

> **USEFUL PHRASES – ASKING FOR AGENDA POINTS AND AGREEMENTS**
>
> Do you have any points you wish to add?
> From our point of view there are some points missing.
> If you have any specific points you would like to include, please …
> Is adding … OK with you?

7 Harold has sent his agenda. However, in the meantime Oracle has received the following letter from Dominions Bank.

Dominions Bank • 1 Upper Bank Street • London E14

The Company Secretary
Oracle Bank
Oracle Square
Riga
Latvia

18 January 2010

Dear Sirs

During our last meeting on 19 December, it was decided to hold a further meeting in the New Year. We have not, as yet, received an agenda from your company. Therefore, we have prepared the enclosed agenda covering the remaining open points. We feel it is in our joint interest to resolve this matter speedily in view of the current worldwide banking crisis.

If there are any areas where you feel no negotiation is necessary, please inform us. If you wish to make any changes to our agenda, or if you have any points you would like to include, please contact the undersigned by 27 January. I can be reached by phone on 0044 020 799966 or by mail at the above address. My email address is mdaniels@dominionsbank.uk.

I look forward to hearing from you.

Yours faithfully

Marisa Daniels

Marisa Daniels, Ms
Chief Financial Officer

AGENDA

Dominions Bank

Agenda for meeting – 11 February
Time: 9.00 am – 5.00 pm
Location: Dominions Bank Board Room, London

Participants
Meeting Chairman – Mr Georgi Borrister M.A.

Dominions Bank	Oracle Bank
Chief Executive Officer Mr Georgi Borrister M.A.	Chief Executive Officer
Chief Financial Officer Ms Marisa Daniels	Chief Financial Officer
Chief Information Officer Mr Donald Hardy	One other Director
Ms Madeline Donaldson P.A. – Minutes	

Topics
- Apologies for absence
- Decisions on amalgamation of headquarters
- Redundancy payments
- Return of company cars
- Branch closures
- Computer amalgamation, supervision by D. Hardy
- Customer issues
- Advertising & branding
- AOB

Now answer the following questions.

1. When was the last meeting with Oracle?

2. What is the date of the new meeting and where will it be held?

3. Has Dominions taken account of any special Oracle Bank issues?

4. What reason did Marisa Daniels give for writing the letter?

5. When is the closing date for new agenda points?

USEFUL PHRASES

Arranging a meeting
I am calling to arrange the … meeting.
Who will be coming from … ?/Who will attend from … ?
Let's meet on/next …
How about … ? Or is … a better time for you?
Could you confirm … in writing, please?

Agreeing the agenda
We need to discuss the agenda …
It is extremely important for us to include …
… has a lower priority.

20 | UNIT 2　Setting objectives

8 **The CFO's secretary at Dominions Bank is ringing Oracle to arrange the meeting in February. Listen and complete the table below.**

	Meeting details
Date:	
Time:	
Place:	

9 **Use the information above to write a formal email from Dominions Bank to Oracle. Confirm the items agreed.**

To: _____
From: _____
Date: _____

Subject: Meeting – Oracle and Dominions' arrangements

Dear _____

_____
_____
_____
_____
_____

Regards
Dominions Bank

THE CULTURAL ICEBERG

There is much more to culture than what we see. Many experts compare it to an iceberg. Like an iceberg, culture is not static. It shifts and drifts around. It has two parts. Above the 'waterline' are behaviours – body language, gestures, actions that we see. However, below the 'waterline' we find values, beliefs, and norms as well as cultural assumptions, which shape the behaviours we see. Understanding culture under the 'waterline' is one key to becoming a successful international negotiator.

---

10 **A British architect is trying to arrange a business meeting for next week with representatives from other countries. These representatives would like to sell their products, i.e. new software for designing houses. Work with a partner.**

PARTNER FILES　Partner A　File 2, p. 70
　　　　　　　　Partner B　File 2, p. 72

OUTPUT

Read the following article.

Getting to know the other side – a Preparation Checklist ✓

'There is no substitute for the hard work of preparation'
(Winston Churchill)

The most difficult aspect in negotiation preparation is finding out about the other side. It is demanding work, but it will pay off in making your negotiation successful and effective. Here are some key points to check off before you start your negotiation:

- ❐ **Do you know *who* the opponent is?** Find out their names and positions. Have you (or members of your team) met them? What else do you know about them?

- ❐ ***Where* does your opponent come from?** Do you know their cultural background, language ability, personal attitudes?

- ❐ **What *experience* does your opponent have?** How did they behave in other negotiations? Are they new in their job(s)? Do they need to prove something?

- ❐ **What *approaches and tactics* did they use in the past?** Can you identify any patterns or characteristics that help you understand them better?

- ❐ **Does the opponent have the *authority*?** Will the agreement stick or does your opponent need permission from someone else?

- ❐ **Do you know what your opponent *wants*?** What are their needs and wants? What are they willing to give in order to reach those needs and wants?

- ❐ **What kind of *pressure* (time, money) is your opponent under?** Does your opponent have a time limit or are they under pressure financially?

- ❐ **What possible *hidden agendas and motives* are there?** What hidden factors might influence them? What motivates them and 'turns them on' or 'off'?

Negotiations take place between people who often view the exact same facts and statements differently. So put yourself in their shoes. Prepare a list of questions you can ask which will help you find out more. Remember, in the words of Richard Nixon, 'Fact-finding is the mother's milk of negotiation.'

OVER TO YOU

- Which three points above do you think are the most important? What other key points would you add to this checklist? Discuss.
- Think about your last negotiations. How much time did you spend on preparation? Would you prepare differently if you did it again?
- Do you agree with Richard Nixon's quote at the end of the checklist? Why, or why not?

3 The meeting

STARTER Which of these suggestions for the early stages of a business meeting do you agree with? Explain why.

- Shake hands and exchange business cards.
- Keep the conversation on business topics only.
- Ask a lot of questions.
- Make notes on the answers given.
- Always be friendly.
- Stay formal.
- Talk about how you feel.

1 A chain of European bookshops, Bookmark PLC, is discussing a distribution contract with Books to Go, a cut-price, American bookstore. Read the cover letter.

To:	Joanna Duncan – Books to Go Corp., New York
From:	Mark Taylor – Bookmark PLC, London
Date:	29 October 2010
Attachment:	Agenda for first organizational meeting
Re:	Final version of the agenda

Dear Ms Duncan

We are writing to confirm that our CEO, Joseph Daniels, has agreed to meet with your directors to discuss distribution possibilities. As you may know, our aim is to internationalize Bookmark's range. We understand that you wish to have a high-profile European presence. Please find attached our proposal for the agenda for this initial meeting.

Following our recent telephone conversation, we suggest that the meeting take place in Paris, as it is a neutral venue. We can then combine this meeting with a visit to the Paris Book Fair, which takes place from 14 to 16 April. We hope that Friday, 13 April is a suitable date for you.

Our directors have a reservation at the Hôtel de Lafayette and we have chosen it as the location for the meeting. A meeting room for a maximum of ten people and two small separate rooms have been reserved for that date.

Our company will act as hosts for the meeting and will therefore cover the costs involved. If you have any queries about this, please contact me on 020 989798 or by email.
I look forward to finally meeting you on 13 April.

Best Regards
Mark Taylor

AGENDA

Participants:
Bookmark PLC
Joseph Daniels – Chairman of the Supervisory Board (will chair meeting)
Rachel Philips – Finance Director
Mark Taylor – Sales Director
Brian Newson – Operations Director
TBA – Minutes

Participants:
Books to Go Corporation
Valentine Stevens – CEO
George East – CFO
Paul Richardson – Sales Director
Dennis Griffith – Website Controller
Joanna Duncan – Personal Assistant (PA) to Mr Stevens

Date and venue
Meeting date: 13 April 2010 at 10:00 am
Venue: Hôtel de Lafayette, Paris

Agenda
10:00   Welcome and short overview of the day (Joseph Daniels)
10:30   Apologies for absence

Coffee
10:45   Short history of company – the possibilities as seen by Joseph Daniels
11:45   Opening statement – review of available titles for Europe – Books to Go

12:45   Lunch in hotel restaurant
14:00   Private meeting for each company in separate rooms

15:00   Return to meeting room – first proposals from each side
17:00   Advertising and website issues
17:30   Initial schedule

Date of next meeting
AOB
Close

2 Using the email and the agenda, answer the following questions.

		Yes	No	Don't know
1	Have Mark and Joanna met before?	☐	☐	☐
2	Has Paris been chosen for the meeting because of the book fair?	☐	☐	☐
3	Is Bookmark based in New York?	☐	☐	☐
4	Will Mark write the minutes of the meeting?	☐	☐	☐
5	Is April 13th OK for all?	☐	☐	☐
6	Is Mr Stevens staying at the Hôtel de Lafayette?	☐	☐	☐

SENDING A COVER LETTER OR EMAIL

Formal opening sentences
I am writing to confirm …
This is to confirm …
Following our telephone conversation …
Following our recent discussions …
Attached you will find …

Formal closing sentences
I look forward to meeting/seeing you …
If you have any queries, please contact me at …
It will be nice to see you at the meeting in/on …
Do not hesitate to contact us if …

3   Put the words in the right order to make sentences that are often used in cover letters.

1   the to confirm meeting this date is the of next

_____

2   the telephone are a following few agenda open there our still points conversation for

_____

3   of summary company a attached financial the you find current will of status the

_____

4   meeting to you topic I with discussing look and the forward you

_____

AMENDING AND CONFIRMING THE AGENDA

Formal questions to confirm details
Could you please confirm that you have received the revised agenda?
Does the agenda meet your needs/expectations?
Do you agree with the other items?
Shall we move forward on this basis?

Closing expressions
I look forward to meeting you.
It will be nice to put a face to a name.

Adding in a final point and justifying it
I believe we will need to speak about … as well.
… has reminded us that we must discuss … because …
It has occurred to us that we need to add … to the agenda.
… must be discussed because …
Could we put … on the agenda after point … ?

A COMPLETE AGENDA TIES UP LOOSE ENDS

At the beginning of the negotiation, go through the agenda and ask for agreement.
A clear agenda that both parties agree to is very helpful in keeping a negotiation effective and concise.

The agenda helps both parties in three ways. It:
- sets a positive atmosphere. It is the first agreement both parties have reached!
- prioritizes the points to be discussed and provides a clear timetable.
- allows both sides to include all points to be discussed.

Don't underestimate the power of the agenda. It saves time and builds the relationship!

UNIT 3 The meeting | 25

4 Mark makes a courtesy telephone call to Joanna. Listen to the conversation and take notes on the notepad below.

5 Listen again and tick the expressions you hear in the second Useful Phrases box on page 24.

6 Put the expressions below in the table. Use the cover email on page 22 to help you.

> 2.30 p.m. • January • … time • … time • the morning • three o'clock • the weekend • lunchtime • the afternoon • 2010 • 4.40 p.m. • Monday

caller – _____

company – _____

comments – _____

contact – _____

at	in	on

7 Fill in the correct prepositions.

1 We will meet _____ Wednesday _____ 5.00 p.m.

2 I am going to see my boss _____ an important matter.

3 I do not like writing emails _____ night.
   In general I prefer working _____ the morning.

4 Where shall we go _____ lunchtime _____ Monday?

5 If you cannot be _____ time, please give me a call.

6 The meeting will be held _____ our headquarters _____ my office _____ Tuesday afternoon.

> The presentation will be **on** Friday **at** 9.00 **in** the morning.
>
> OK, I'll make sure everyone arrives **at** the conference centre **on** time.

8 Arrange an appointment with a partner to discuss business. Plan the call by following the flow diagram. Do not forget to practise some small talk.

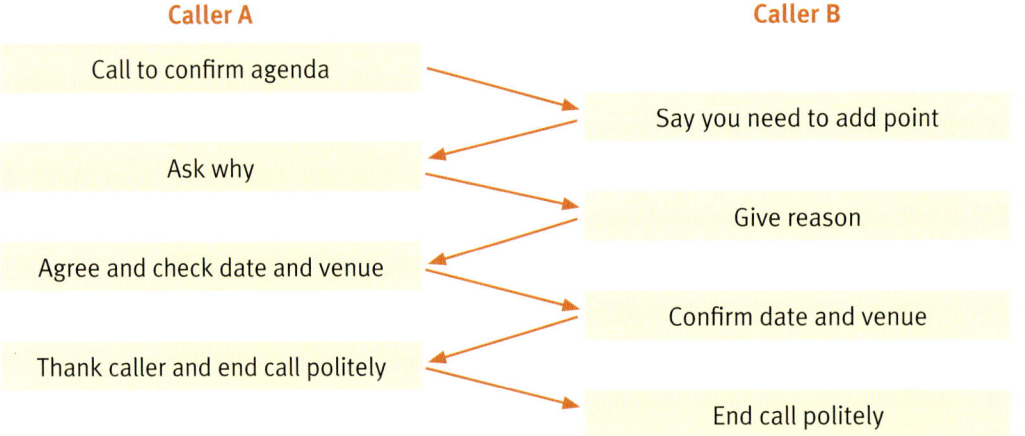

 9 Bookmark and Books to Go each discuss their aims for the meeting. Listen to each meeting and answer the questions below.

1 What are Bookmark's main goals for the meeting?
_____

2 What are Books to Go's main objectives?
_____

3 Do they have any conflicting aims?
_____

4 Which company has financial problems?
_____

5 Which company has a problem with unsold older books?
_____

10 Match the sentence parts. Which sentence is said by which company? Write 'B' for Bookmark and 'BTG' for Books to Go.

_____ 1 If we increase the range of stock available,   a I won't insist on including fiction as well.
_____ 2 If we say we've already covered all the costs,   b it will help with sales.
_____ 3 If they give us a good deal on our list of non-fiction,   c we'll let them sell their books in our stores.
_____ 4 If they work with us on the website,   d they might not want to contribute.
_____ 5 If we can get a quick agreement,   e that should help.

UNIT **3** The meeting | **27**

> **MAKE YOUR GOALS REAL**
>
> Define your goals! The clearer they are, the easier it is to reach them. In addition, be sure to let the other party know exactly what you want.
>
> Here are four questions you can ask yourself to check how REAL your goals are.
> Can you **R**ate them?   *How important are the goals? – What priorities do they follow?*
> Are they **E**xact?   *How clearly defined are the goals? – Can you measure them?*
> Are they **A**chievable?   *How realistic are the goals? – Can they be reached in the time frame?*
> Are they **L**ogical?   *Do the goals make sense for both parties?*

11 **Bookmark and Books to Go start to develop a good relationship. Listen to the beginning of the meeting between Bookmark and Books to Go and answer the following questions.**

1 What is Mr Griffith's job at the bookstore?
___

2 What does Mr Newson do?
___

3 Why does he say he used to work for Mega-Online?
___

4 Have Mr Daniels and Mr Stevens met before?
___

12 **Listen again to how the participants are introduced. Tick the phrases you hear in the box below.**

> **MEETING AND GREETING**
>
> How do you do? (answered with 'How do you do?')
> Very pleased to meet you.
> It is a pleasure to meet you …
> May I introduce … He/She is …
> This is … He/She heads our …
> Have you met … ?
> I don't think you have met …

13 **Write a few short sentences about yourself and give them to a partner. Take it in turns to introduce each other using the expressions above.**

___
___
___

14 Read the Chairman's welcoming speech and fill in the gaps with the words below.

> come up with • fall in with • go along with • look forward to • put up

Bookmark PLC

Mr Joseph Daniels – Chairman of the Supervisory Board
Venue: Hôtel de Lafayette, Paris

Chairman's speech

Good morning ladies and gentlemen. It's my great pleasure to welcome you to our first meeting. I hope you had good flights and you've all managed to check into your hotels, where I'm sure you will be well looked after. We have _____ [1] all our guests in an excellent hotel and I think most of the local hotels have _____ [2] some good ideas to make a business traveller's stay satisfactory.

I hope you can all _____ [3] the agenda, which was circulated and agreed before the meeting. We feel the meeting should be held in a friendly and co-operative spirit, and hope that you can all _____ [4] our decision to take these values forward into the new venture. This attitude will, I believe, be beneficial for our business and I _____ [5] our co-operation.

15 Match the expressions with their meanings.

	Expressions		Meanings
1	go along with	a	think of
2	fall in with	b	set up in hotel
3	look forward to	c	not argue against
4	put up	d	anticipate
5	come up with	e	accept

Answers:

1 ☐ 2 ☐ 3 ☐ 4 ☐ 5 ☐

EXCHANGING BUSINESS CARDS

The way business cards are exchanged varies from country to country and can set the tone for the rest of the business relationship. When someone hands you their business card, make a good impression! Take the card while thanking the person. Then read the card, before putting it away. It not only shows that you are interested; it also gives you a chance to learn something about the person and the company, which, in turn, may help you to understand the person better! If you grab the card and simply place it into your pocket, you may show disrespect.

16 A buyer and seller in the fashion industry arrange to meet. First call to set up the final agenda for the meeting. Then, before the meeting, introduce yourself to the people who you have not met beforehand.

PARTNER FILES Partner A File 3, p. 70
Partner B File 3, p. 72

OUTPUT

Read the following article by Dr Stanley Carter, a bank director in London.

Leave money on the negotiating table!

Here are five key tips to help you lose money, confuse your own team and help the other party gain the advantage at the negotiating table:

1 Avoid making an agenda

The last thing you want is for both sides to know about what points come next. There's plenty of time for chatting about whatever comes to mind – especially when the other party asks you what you want to talk about. They will be impressed by your flexibility.

2 Go into the negotiation unprepared

Preparation is a waste of time. Besides, you already know everything there is to know. It doesn't make any difference who else is at the table. You have your price and terms. They simply will have to take it or leave it. Your conditions are the best anyway. And, of course, you'll impress your boss with the ability to think on your feet.

3 Alternatives only complicate the negotiation

Be sure to stick to your one and only goal, no matter what! Finding alternatives to the problem only makes the whole negotiation more complicated, extends the length of the negotiation and keeps you away from more important problems at your desk. Don't consider any alternatives from the other party, either! They're only trying to hide something from you and obscure the issue at hand.

4 Focus on your own interests

Don't worry about listening to what the other party wants or needs! It's only important that you reach your goal, regardless of what they want. Above all, don't ask any questions! This just brings in more details, which will distract you from your goal.

Remember, time is money. So get directly and immediately to your goal. Interrupt if you have to. It's not important what the other side says, anyway.

5 Avoid clear roles

Always have at least five members of your team at the negotiation table! The more, the better! But be sure that everyone speaks – preferably at the same time! Save time beforehand by first discussing your internal viewpoints while at the table and not before. But be sure to whisper, so that the other party doesn't hear what you're saying. Remember also to keep key information from your own members for as long as possible. They will applaud you on your ability to keep a secret.

OVER TO YOU

- What tips would you give to help someone negotiate successfully?
- Think about a negotiation that broke down or became very difficult. What caused it and how could it have been avoided?
- When can you go into a negotiation without preparing properly? Defend your opinion.

4 Proposals

STARTER Imagine you are organizing the company summer party with a colleague. You discuss all the things that can make this day a success. Check the notepad and pick your favourite items.

- **theme**: Asian ☐, Latin American ☐, Western ☐
- **location**: at work ☐, on a ship ☐, formal venue ☐
- **entertainment**: colleagues' band ☐, professional group ☐, disco ☐
- **type of food**: finger food ☐, barbecue ☐, formal meal ☐
- **attire/dress code**: casual ☐, formal ☐, fancy dress ☐
- **budget**: company sponsored ☐, purchased tickets ☐
- **time of year**: summer ☐, winter ☐, spring ☐

Compare your notes with a partner. Did you have much in common or do you have to negotiate a lot of items?

PROPOSAL VS. COUNTERPROPOSAL

A **proposal** is an offer made by one party to the other. Proposals can be made in written and/or verbal form. They provide the basis for the negotiation and a possible settlement, i.e. the deal. A successful proposal is one that results in an agreement.

A **counterproposal** offers an alternative proposal that may suit both parties. This can happen when one party refuses or does not agree with the original proposal.

UNIT 4 Proposals | 31

1 Listen to the following negotiation. Some of the points mentioned in the discussion are listed below. Tick 'P' if the statement is a proposal, and 'CP' for a counterproposal.

		P	CP
1	One shipment for all the goods	☐	☐
2	Production time of 15 working days and four days for transportation	☐	☐
3	Pick-up by customer	☐	☐
4	Part-shipment	☐	☐
5	Delivery by air freight	☐	☐
6	Delivery of three (not four) shipments	☐	☐
7	Working longer hours	☐	☐
8	Production time of 15 working days and two days for transportation	☐	☐

Agenda

- apologies for absence
- delivery time for containers
- delivery terms
- price
- confidentiality agreement

2 Read the transcript of the meeting on page 82. Underline the proposal and circle the two counterproposals. Share your list with the rest of the class.

PRESENTING PROPOSALS AND COUNTERPROPOSALS	ASKING FOR AND CLARIFYING INFORMATION
I/We propose …	… is correct, isn't it?
I/We suggest …	Can you tell me how … ?
How about … ?	Is it alright with you if … ?
Would it be possible … ?	Would it be possible … ?
How do you feel about … ?	It seems … What is your opinion?
Would/Could you consider … ?	
Would/Could you accept … ?	

3 Are the statements below true (✓) or false (✗)? Listen again and check your answers.

		T	F
1	The initial offer stated 25 days for production and four days' delivery time.	☐	☐
2	A proposal was made to produce the goods within ten working days.	☐	☐
3	A further proposal was to work two shifts instead of three.	☐	☐
4	An alternative was part-shipments at seven-day intervals.	☐	☐
5	Delivery of amounts in fewer shipments was suggested.	☐	☐
6	One shipment for the whole amount was discussed.	☐	☐

4 Rewrite the statements in exercise 3 using the Useful Phrases on page 31.

Example: Would you consider a production time of 25 working days?
Would it be possible to produce within 25 working days?

1 _____   4 _____

2 _____   5 _____

3 _____

REWARD VERBAL SIGNALS

In every negotiation there are both verbal and non-verbal signals. A gesture is a non-verbal signal. A statement, on the other hand, is a verbal signal. When you say 'Yes, I am interested', you send a verbal signal. It can be a very clear and direct proposal ('How about a 5% increase?'), or it can be a hidden and indirect statement ('I'm afraid that's not possible at the moment', which means 'Perhaps we could talk about this later'). Some verbal signals (e.g. 'Hmm!') just show that you are listening to the other speaker.

In any case, it is important to listen carefully and react properly to verbal signals if you want the negotiation to progress efficiently and successfully. Don't ignore them! Send and reward them! They help intensify your business relationship.

5 Marcy has a lot to think about because the discussions were rather complicated. Help Marcy clarify her thoughts. Write her a note with all your ideas in complete sentences.

Then practise presenting your proposals and asking for clarification with a partner.

6 Put the words in the right order to make questions.

1 order could increasing by imagine amount you 10% the ?
   _____

2 you order 500 how per feel do pieces about ?
   _____

3 are you how goods can stored me the tell ?
   _____

4 by about rail of how truck instead by transport ?
   _____

5 container with is load a in alright if you we it ?
   _____

6 alternative an freight be would sea ?
   _____

7 your part-shipment a is on opinion what ?
   _____

7 The meeting continues. Listen to the conversation and fill in the gaps with the words you hear.

Jason … That's right. This morning we _____[1] earlier delivery, part-shipment, an additional shift, and increased order quantities. We have looked at each alternative very carefully. We are _____[2] a third shift.

Marcy Well, I guessed you wouldn't want that, because of the increase in price. However, it is a solution if there is a major increase in demand which needs to be met quickly.

Jason At the moment, this is _____[3] to happen. But who knows?

Marcy There is also the possibility of shipping the goods at intervals. What do you think of that?

Jason Unfortunately, that is _____[4] either, because once again we would be looking at a price increase. Transport is really getting more and more costly these days!

Marcy True, but that depends, then, on which forwarder you use. _____[5] I would be able to help you negotiate a very good price with our forwarder. Would you like me to try? I'm sure he'll be interested in dealing with you.

Jason Of course! If you think that _____[6] that. But we would have to look at that again at a later date, though.

Marcy OK, I've made a note of it and we'll let you know.

Jason Thank you, Marcy. Good. Now Craig wants to discuss the final proposal with you. Craig?

Craig Your question was about storage capacity. _____⁷ do it. We have checked and with a little careful planning we could store three containers.

Marcy Good to hear. However, I have another suggestion. There is also the possibility of adjusting order quantities according to your needs. Let's say, three containers in one shipment as discussed, two in another, or even four, if necessary. This would be OK as long as we stick to the overall order quantities we agreed to.

Craig That is a nice offer. But _____⁸ store four containers unless we build another warehouse and _____⁹. Still ... ordering two containers is an alternative, should there be any changes.

USEFUL PHRASES

Expressing possibilities/probabilities
It is possible/probable/conceivable (that) ...
There is a possibility (that) ...
It may be ...
It could well be that ...
In all probability ...
It is to be expected ...

Expressing impossibilities/improbabilities
It is impossible to ...
It is out of the question ...
Unfortunately, that cannot be done!
We can rule out the possibility of ...
It is doubtful whether/if ...
It is (hardly) likely ...

8 Read the following conversation. Fill in the gaps with words from the box.

alternative • alternative • doubtful • expect • expectation • imagine • opinion • possibility • possible • proposal • propose • question • unfortunately • unlikely

A In order to meet your _____¹ about the price, can you _____² an increase in order quantity of 25%?

B No, _____³, we cannot. We did, however, _____⁴ an increase by 10% last week.

A Was that your _____⁵?

B Yes, it was, because it is _____⁶ if it is _____⁷ for us to store more.

A An _____⁸ would be to deliver the goods at shorter intervals.

B To be honest, it is _____⁹ that we will favour that _____¹⁰.

A Another _____¹¹ would be to store the goods at a lower price and call off the order when needed. What is your _____¹²?

B That is out of the _____¹³.

A OK, then, what exactly do you _____¹⁴.

UNIT 4 Proposals | 35

9 Now find the words used in the gaps in exercise 8 in the wordsearch.

P	D	O	U	B	T	F	U	L	I	K	E	L	Y	Z
O	I	D	I	F	L	I	P	N	P	Y	T	H	E	N
S	S	M	M	O	T	W	R	U	L	E	O	U	T	O
S	T	I	A	D	E	P	O	S	S	I	B	L	E	T
I	I	D	G	G	U	M	P	L	O	N	K	S	S	E
B	N	C	I	N	I	P	O	P	E	N	T	E	N	F
I	C	A	N	I	T	N	S	V	Q	U	A	W	L	A
L	T	M	A	Y	E	N	E	X	P	E	C	T	O	Y
I	A	L	T	E	R	N	A	T	I	V	E	N	T	A
T	M	P	I	B	O	P	I	N	I	O	N	O	U	N
Y	P	R	O	P	O	S	A	L	E	Z	V	C	L	L
T	A	U	N	F	O	R	T	U	N	A	T	E	L	Y
O	Q	X	R	E	Q	U	E	S	T	I	O	N	E	S
P	E	X	P	E	C	T	A	T	I	O	N	C	E	W

> **THE POWER OF BATNA**
>
> The expression **BATNA** was invented by R. Fisher and W. Ury in their book *Getting to Yes*. It stands for **B**est **A**lternative **T**o a **N**egotiated **A**greement. It means that you know what you will do if you do not reach an agreement. The clearer your BATNA is to you, the stronger you will be at the negotiating table, because you will be able to demand from the other party exactly what you want. The principal advantage of knowing your BATNA is that you will know when to stop negotiating! However, also estimate your opponent's BATNA – and you'll estimate their power, too.

10 During the lunch break Jason, Richard, and Craig discuss the current status of the negotiation via email. Read their correspondence and complete the missing information using Jason's notes.

Notes

- 15 days for production until dispatch
  - 10 production days until dispatch???
  - Not possible because of set-up time, checks!!!!
  - Alternatives?
- 4 working days' shipping time
  - Not a lot we can do!
- 3 shifts instead of 2?
  - Possible, but what about the price?
  - Too expensive, no doubt!
- Part-shipment every 7 days
  - Transport costs? Shall we check?
- Storage capacity
  - How much can we store?
- 3 containers ...
  - Should (Can we) cut transport time and save money?
  - Can the material be stored safely for longer periods?
  - Production would run more smoothly.
  - Allows forward planning.

Hi there

Before we go back to the meeting, please take a look at the notes I've written up so far!

I feel that the meeting is going rather well. What do you think? Everybody seems to be comfortable and we have already agreed on one major point. We got what we wanted. What more can you ask?

Unfortunately, there is some disagreement on the delivery and we should look at the alternatives before we decide if we can work something out that will suit both sides.

1 In my opinion, there is _____[1] we can do about _____[2]. Production time remains at _____[3] unless we ask them to work _____[4]. If we do that, then we'll have to consider the price increase. Shift allowances are expensive.

2 Are part-shipments really an option for us? If they are, then would _____[5] be a problem?

3 Delivery of _____[6] is certainly my favourite solution. If we agree to that, then we can _____[7]. The question is: can we store the material safely for longer periods? If storage is possible, then production would _____[8] and that would help us with _____[9] in the future.

How do you feel about it?

If possible, please let me have your answer by 1 pm. Hopefully we can find a viable alternative before we return to the meeting.

Jason

11 It is 12.30 p.m. and you finally have time to study the proposals. Write an answer to Jason and let him know what you think. Do you agree with Jason?

To: Jason
From: _____
Subject: Today's meeting

_____
_____
_____
_____
_____
_____

UNIT **4** Proposals | **37**

> **EXPRESSING CONDITIONS AND POSSIBLE RESULTS**
>
> We often use *if* sentences to express requirements and their possible results.
>
> | **Requirements** | **Possible results** |
> |---|---|
> | '**If** we agree to that, | **then** we can save time and money.' |
> | '**If** there is space, | **then** we can store more goods.' |
> | '**If** I leave now, | **then** I will be able to catch the bus.' |

12 Read Jason's email again. Find the sentences using 'if' and underline them.

13 Below is a list of requirements and possible results. Match the requirements (1–7) to the possible results (a–g). Then write your answers in complete sentences.

requirement		possible result
1 ... win the lottery ...		a ... prepare the presentations myself.
2 ... get the work done ...		b ... three shifts a day.
3 ... get the order ...		c ... work all weekend.
4 ... go to the meeting in London ...		d ... stop working.
5 ... do the research ...		e ... save a lot of money.
6 ... attend a PowerPoint course ...		f ... visit the trade fair.
7 ... all go together ...		g ... go home early.

1 _____
2 _____
3 _____
4 _____
5 _____
6 _____
7 _____

If we work through the weekend, then we'll be ready for the meeting on Monday.

... then I won't be able to go to Paris.

... then I can't go to the dentist after all!

UNIT 4 Proposals

14 A year and a half later, Richard is visiting Marcy in order to look at the new production line. They are discussing their successful business partnership. He takes this opportunity to ask some important questions. Rewrite the questions below using the Useful Phrases on page 34 and answer the questions on Marcy's behalf.

Richard: Can we reduce transportation time by sea freight from six to four weeks?

(impossible/because/shipping routes)

1 Richard _____
2 Marcy _____

Richard: Do you think we can have a further discount of 2.5%?

(because/price/unfortunately/raw materials)

3 Richard _____
4 Marcy _____

Richard: Is the price increasing on the commodities market?

(will/increase/price/year)

5 Richard _____
6 Marcy _____

Richard: Will there be a shortage of container space on ships in the near future?

(because/volume/export/rise)

7 Richard _____
8 Marcy _____

Richard: Is the exchange rate staying at its current level?

(due to/continue/decline/stay/dollar)

9 Richard _____
10 Marcy _____

Richard: Are you opening another production plant?

(available/because/no/suitable/property)

11 Richard _____
12 Marcy _____

Now listen to the correct answers.

UNIT 4 Proposals

15 **Work with a partner. Make up questions with the information below. Then answer these questions by using the Useful Phrases on page 34.**

> borrow your car • finish production tomorrow • build a new production hall
> • have fabric in pink • speak to the boss • check stock levels for the product
> • double delivery quantity

Example: Do you think I can borrow your car?
Borrowing my car is out of the question!

1 _____
2 _____
3 _____
4 _____
5 _____
6 _____

AVOID THE PITFALLS OF BODY LANGUAGE

Body language can never be absolutely straightforward. There are three reasons.

1 A gesture may be physical and have no psychological meaning. If you scratch your nose, you may be feeling dishonest, uncomfortable – or it may be that you just have an itch.

2 The interpretation of a gesture is often very vague. You may notice that when someone touches their face, it is a sign of nervousness. But nervousness about what? Only the context can tell you.

3 People are not naïve. They may deliberately change their body language to convey the impression they want to give.

16 **A car dealer is discussing the sale of a fleet of cars for a new company customer.**

PARTNER FILES Partner A File 4, p. 70
Partner B File 4, p. 73

OUTPUT Read the questionnaire. Tick the most appropriate phrase. Add the points and check your score.

Results or relationships?
Get the deal or build trust?

What kind of negotiator are you? Do you feel it's more important to have a good relationship with the other party or is it more important to win the contract? For most people, building a relationship and getting the deal are important aspects of an effective negotiation.

1 How important are your feelings in a negotiation?
- [ ] a If I reveal my true feelings, the other party will take advantage of them.
- [ ] b I don't consider the consequences my feelings may have on my opponent.
- [ ] c I hide my feelings from my opponent by using the correct body language.

2 What priority does building a relationship have in a negotiation?
- [ ] a Keeping a good relationship is more important than making somebody angry by rejecting a marginally acceptable deal.
- [ ] b A good relationship is essential in any negotiation.
- [ ] c My interests are more important than building a relationship.

3 When is it important to close a deal?
- [ ] a A marginally acceptable deal is better than no deal at all.
- [ ] b 'Something for nothing' is always better than 'something for something'.
- [ ] c I look after my interests, but I also look after theirs, too.

4 How do you deal with how the other party views you?
- [ ] a I don't worry about rejection when negotiating.
- [ ] b I am willing to give in when a relationship is important.
- [ ] c If the other party lets me take advantage of a situation, then I do.

5 What role does power play for you?
- [ ] a It is best to be open about true intentions.
- [ ] b If the other party is under pressure, I push harder.
- [ ] c Power is more important than a good cause.

What kind of negotiator are you?

1–5 points:
You are concerned with relationships and you seek co-operation. Your target is to win the war, even if it means losing the battle. But be careful, or you may be taken advantage of.

6–10 points:
You believe that a negotiated outcome can benefit both sides. You place value on both relationship and results. Remember that preparation is still key!

11–15 points:
You are concerned more with results than with relationships. In order for one party to win, the other may have to lose. You prefer to take something for less than you give.

Your score:
1 a–1;b–3;c–2 2 a–2;b–1;c–3 3 a–1;b–1;c–3 4 a–3;b–1;c–2 5 a–1;b–2;c–3

5 A new offer

You share an office with a colleague. It is quite cold outside, but the heater is set to mark 3 and you feel comfortable. When you return from your lunch break, you notice that the room is very warm. You check the radiator and see that it has been turned up. You turn the radiator down again. Five minutes later, your colleague gets up and turns it back up, and ...

- What do you think happens next?
- How would you go about finding a solution?
- Is it possible for each of you to 'win'?

1 Dwight Robinson heads the Department of International Sales at Nacatomi Corporation. He is one of the most innovative managers in the company and played a major role in making Nacatomi successful. He wants to negotiate a pay raise with his boss, Mr Yamamoto.

Listen to their conversation and fill in the gaps for the five statements below.

1 _____ my first pay raise in more than four years.

2 _____ that we can come to an agreement. Unfortunately, though, I just cannot agree to 10%!

3 _____ for this. If you remember, none of the staff have had a pay raise in the last four years because business has been difficult.

4 _____ a higher pay raise?

5 So, _____ you correctly, you are telling me that I can take it or leave it?

Now listen again and check your answers.

UNIT 5 A new offer

2 Turn to the transcript on pages 83–84. Underline the expressions used in the dialogue to *clarify information* and circle the language used to *express opinions*.

> **USEFUL PHRASES**
>
> **Clarifying information**
> Do you suggest … ?
> Are you suggesting that … ?
> Do you mean … ?
> Does that mean … ?
> If I understand you correctly … ?
> What do you mean by … ?
>
> **Expressing opinions**
> In my/our opinion …
> From my/our point of view …
> We are talking/speaking about …
> I am/We are of the opinion that …
> I/We strongly believe/feel that …
> I am confident that …
> I/We imagine it's something like …

3 In Unit 4 we looked at proposals and counterproposals. There are two counterproposals in the dialogue. What are they?

1 _____

2 _____

Now make two new proposals which clarify and express your opinion. Use the expressions above.

1 _____

2 _____

4 Complete the sentences on page 43 with the phrases below.

A:
Another option would be …
I imagine it's something like …
Are you suggesting … ?

B:
Does that mean … ?
We are talking about …
Do you think we can … ?

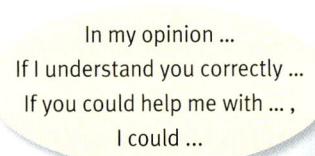

C:
In my opinion …
If I understand you correctly …
If you could help me with … ,
I could …

1 Buying a new car? _____, a new engine is still cheaper than a new car!

2 Round? That is expensive, but _____ a square one only cheaper.

3 Not enough information? _____ I have to give a more detailed explanation?

4 I understand you think it's expensive! _____ to make it smaller.

5 It can't be fixed? _____, you are telling me that I need a new computer.

6 Oh dear, _____ completely rewriting the documentation for the course.

7 More feedback? _____ split the work between three people instead?

8 Something cheaper? _____ looking for a different type of material?

9 _____ this matter, _____ sort the cheque out straight away.

5 Underline the *correct* phrase in the sentences.

1 **If I understand you correctly / Are you proposing / Do you suggest** to help out at the meeting?

2 **We are talking about / We are confident / We believe** the goods are faulty.

3 **Does that mean / In my opinion / Do you suggest** we have to move to Nottingham?

4 **Do you suggest / In our opinion / Do you mean** you will check on the details?

5 **Do you think / We strongly believe / I imagine it something like** we can work this out.

6 **We feel that / We are of the opinion that / We are talking** about an increase of 10%.

BARGAINING VS. NEGOTIATING

Hard Bargaining: In hard bargaining, each party tries to achieve their aims without making concessions or making only few or small ones. The aim is to 'beat' the other side. This style leads to a win–lose scenario, i.e. one side wins and the other loses. Often, the result is a stalemate, which results in a lose–lose situation.

Soft Bargaining: In soft bargaining, the parties try to reach an agreement by giving concessions very freely. The soft bargainer often makes proposals very quickly and says 'yes' rather soon. This type of negotiator is often afraid of hurting the other party's feelings.

Principled Negotiating: In their book, *Getting to Yes*, Fisher and Ury introduced this term. It refers to a style which focuses on discovering the interests behind the position. The principled negotiator separates the person from the issue and concentrates on mutual gain in order to reach agreement. In short, it leaves both sides with a sense of achievement, i.e. a win–win situation.

Read the dialogue in exercise 1 again. In your opinion, what kind of negotiation style is used here? Soft, hard, or principled? Why do you think so?

6 **Dwight is thinking about possible alternatives to the 10% pay raise he asked for. He contacts Warren, a tax advisor. Unfortunately, Dwight spilt some coffee on the printout.**

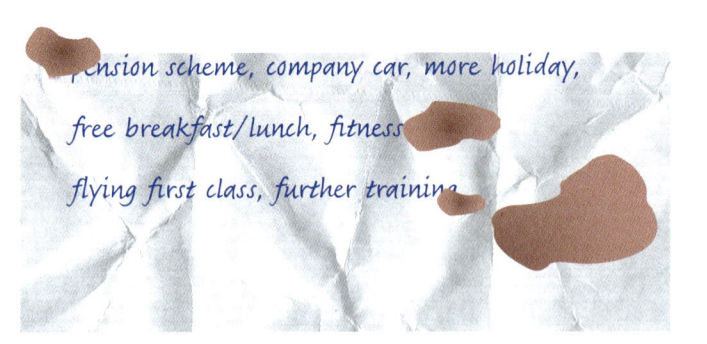

pension scheme, company car, more holiday,
free breakfast/lunch, fitness
flying first class, further training

Read Warren's reply and complete the printout with the words from the box.

breakfast • company • holiday • payment • present • suggest

Subject: HELP!!!!!!!!   2010-05-09   15:29
To: dwight.robinson@nacatomi-corp.com
From: w.miller@tax-advisors.org

Dear Dwight

I have thought about some things you can _____ ¹ to your employer. Sort them into priorities and _____ ² the best two. If you don't mention them all, then you will leave yourself room to manoeuvre. I hope these help.

– Additional monthly _____ ³ of 3.5% into the pension scheme. These payments are fully tax-deductible.

– _____ ⁴ car can be used privately. You have to pay tax and social insurance contributions on the value of your annual private mileage.

– Three extra days' paid _____ ⁵. N_____ot li_____ll.

– Language course paid for by the company. It will help in everyday business and can be set off against taxes.

– _____ ⁶ and luncheon vouchers for the canteen. Again tax-deductible. N___
A_____g on _____ food bill, but _____ d of ti___

– Use of the fitness and childcare facilities for free or, alternatively, subsidized. The tax office allows a deduction here, too.

– As for the holiday in Spain and a first-class flight ... I would NOT suggest it!!!!

Best regards
Warren

UNIT **5** A new offer | 45

> **USEFUL PHRASES**
>
> **Responding to proposals**
> There are several options …
> That would depend on …
> Now that you mention it, …
> Considering this, I/we would …
> It sounds like an alternative option/possibility …
>
> **Suggesting solutions**
> I/We could imagine …
> I/We think we should …
> I was/We were thinking that …
> It would be helpful/an option …
> It might be possible to/a possibility …
> From my/our experience, the best way …
> Do you think we can/could … ?
> Could the problem be solved by … ?

7 Look at Warren's information again. Help Dwight rewrite the email. Use the box above.

To: H. Yamamoto
From: D. Robinson
Subject: Proposals

Dear Mr Yamamoto

Further to our conversation, and as agreed, here are several possible options:

1. ☐ Additional monthly payment of 3.5% into a pension scheme.

2. ☐ Company car can be used privately.

3. ☐ Three more days' paid holiday.

4. ☐ Language course can be paid for by company.

5. ☐ Breakfast and lunch vouchers can be provided for the canteen.

6. ☐ Use of the fitness and childcare facilities for free or, alternatively, subsidized.

I have received the information from your secretary. I am available and am looking forward to our conference on Friday at 10.30 am.

Best regards
D. Robinson

Dwight's friend, Warren, suggested ordering these statements according to priority. Which of the alternatives would be at the top of your list? Rank them and explain why.

8 After further consideration, Dwight has decided not to send his email. Instead he just decides to present his top two choices to Mr Yamamoto. Look again at Warren's information. How would you order the statements? Help Dwight make his two first choices and rewrite the email.

To: H. Yamamoto
From: D. Robinson
Subject: Proposals

Dear Mr Yamamoto
As discussed and agreed, I would like to present the following alternatives:

1 _____
  _____

2 _____
  _____

I am available and am looking forward to our forthcoming conference on Friday at 10.30 am.

Best regards
D. Robinson

LEADERSHIP IN MULTICULTURAL TEAMS

In a multicultural team there are three basic difficulties a leader faces. They are:

1 **Task conflict**: Different cultures can view a task differently. For this reason, it is important to clarify the task, outline its particular features and the intended results.
2 **Procedural conflict**: Difficulties can arise due to differing conceptions throughout the world with respect to hierarchy, communication styles and problem-solving guidelines. Therefore, how the job is done must be clearly defined and agreed to throughout the project.
3 **Interpersonal conflict**: Social identity is key. People who look similar to us, speak like us and agree with our views reinforce our identity. Interpersonal conflict arises when we lose face in front of people of a similar background. This may threaten our social identity.

As a result, keep in mind that information sharing, common understanding and management support are essential in order to achieve success.

---

9 Put the words in the right order to make phrases.

1 able work to We out were things _____ ☐

2 get to business us Let down _____ ☐

3 certainly It an would alternative to be … _____ ☐

4 alternatives far So three established have we … _____ ☐

5 two but you We have imagine possibilities could … _____ ☐

6 option sounds my In like opinion that an _____ ☐

AUDIO 13

Now mark the sentences according to the order you hear them.

UNIT **5** A new offer | **47**

10 It is Friday, 10.30 a.m. Listen to the conversation between Dwight and Mr Yamamoto and decide if the following statements are true (✓) or false (✗).

1. Dwight would like an additional monthly payment into his savings account.
2. Mr Yamamoto proposes a holiday in Spain.
3. Dwight wants to use the company car and pay tax and social security on the mileage.
4. Mr Yamamoto thinks that a language course is a good alternative.
5. Mr Yamamoto agrees to Dwight's initial proposal of 10%.
6. They agree on an additional payment into the pension scheme.

> **UNCOVERING INTERESTS**
>
> If you want to succeed in a negotiation, find out as much as you can about the needs and concerns that underlie a party's position. Clearly, different interests will generate different results.
>
> Therefore, be aware of the following:
> - Cultural background affects the relative importance of specific points. Know as much as possible about the culture of the party you're dealing with.
> - Don't underestimate the importance of particular interests for the other party. Interests are the reason why claims are made and rejected.
> - Use questions (i.e. *who, what, when, where, why, how*) to gather information on interests.

11 In the table below there is a list of problems which you have to solve. The proposals are made by your counterpart. Alternative I shows your proposals. Think of another alternative, and enter it in Alternative II. Prepare your statements and present them to the class.

	Problem	Proposal	Alternative I	Alternative II
1	Delivery quantity too big	Return excess amount	Keep excess amount at 25% discount	1
2	Car is silver instead of black	Keep the car and get three free inspections	Wait eight weeks for a black car	2
3	The tailor damaged your dress/suit	Make an identical dress/suit	Repair the damage at no cost	3
4	You want a pay raise of 5%	A pay raise of 3%	1.5% pay raise and a company car	4
5	A fault with your new computer	A new computer	Find the fault and repair it	5
6	Delivery time too long	Deliver larger quantities	Working three shifts instead of two	Deliver at regular intervals
7	Price of goods is too high	Reduce price by 7.5%	Order larger quantities	6

Example: 1 Our objective is to reduce the delivery time.
We need to reduce delivery time.
2 You propose the delivery of larger quantities.
How about delivering at regular intervals?

Now think of a problem you had to solve in the past and how you did it. Explain it to a partner.

12 Synonyms are words and phrases that can be used in place of other words. Find the synonyms for the following words and place them in the box below.

Example: That sounds like an *alternative/option* or *choice*.

> aim • belief • goal • position • proposal • quotation • target •
> to determine • to forecast • to go up • to identify • to look up • to investigate
> • to project • to raise • to recommend • to resolve • to suggest • to tackle

		Synonyms	
	offer	quotation	proposal
1	to propose		
2	to increase		
3	to predict		
4	to establish		
5	opinion		
6	to research		
7	objective		
8	to solve		

13 Rewrite the statements using the synonyms above for the following words.

1 This _____ is now two months old. (offer)
2 Can you _____ the problem? (solve)
3 Sales have _____ by 10%. (increase)
4 We have _____ the facts. (establish)
5 I _____ looking for a different supplier. (propose)
6 Our _____ is to lower costs. (objective)
7 Mike wants _____ the material. (to research)
8 We _____ that the price will go up. (predict)
9 It is our _____ that this offer cannot be beaten. (opinion)

14 A member of a trade union and an employers' association meet to negotiate new conditions.

PARTNER FILES Partner A File 5, p. 71
Partner B File 5, p. 73

Get behind a position to create a win–win scenario – a true story

HealthySkin Ltd., a large international company in the field of healthcare, was interested in expanding its business. For this reason, it approached ZSC GmbH, a research and development unit in Germany, and expressed interest in a new healthcare product ingredient, which ZSC was working on. The parties sat down to negotiate the deal and very quickly agreed on a price of €32 per kilo for 500,000 kilos a year. However, one problem remained. ZSC would not agree to sell exclusively to HealthySkin. In addition, HealthySkin would not invest in the new product if their competition had access to this particular ingredient.

Neither side was willing to budge with respect to this key point. Due to the question of exclusivity it looked, unfortunately, like the deal was going to fall through. Recognizing the deadlock, HealthySkin decided to bring Doug Skeen into the negotiation to help find a way out of this impasse and solve the problem. Doug, well-trained in dealing with dispute negotiations, had to find an alternative, which was acceptable to both parties.

Doug's first step was not to argue the position of exclusivity. This had not brought the parties forward. Instead he asked questions about why there was resistance and what motivated each party's position. He wanted to understand their reasons.

Soon he discovered that ZSC really wanted to do business with HealthySkin. In fact, they felt that €32 per kilo was a very fair price and were happy that HealthySkin was going to buy almost the whole quantity ZSC produced. But Doug also found out that ZSC had a prior agreement with a small company, Thompson & Co., for 150 kilos a year for a locally-sold product. This was the reason why ZSC could not grant HealthySkin exclusivity. It had nothing to do with HeathySkin's major competitors.

Once each party's reasons were known, it was soon clear that their interests were not really in conflict with each other. As a result, they began discussions again and a deal was quickly reached. HealthySkin was granted exclusivity except for the couple of hundred kilos for Thompson & Co. Thanks to Doug's expertise, both HealthySkin and ZSC were able to come to a win–win solution.

OVER TO YOU

- Think about a negotiation situation you were in where you were arguing your position. Could it have been made win–win? How?
- Why do parties get into arguments? Are arguments a part of negotiations, or should they always be avoided?
- What other suggestions could you give to help solve a conflict?

6 Dealing with deadlock

STARTER Read the following text.

Dealing with deadlock – Negotiation tactics

A good negotiator's aim is to reach a **win–win situation** and a **deal**. However, in business it is not always possible to take the direct route. Often you may find that you need to address minor problems first in order to avoid **stalemate**.

Here are some useful tips:
- Listen to the other party's explanations actively and respectfully.
- Avoid unnecessary **confrontation**. Don't get into **arguments**.
- Hold back on your reactions and stay focused. Ignore **attacks**.
- Deal with the **impasse** together. Accept criticism, but rephrase it in a less confrontational style. Try to see the reasons behind the **standstill** and look for **solutions**.
- Avoid **escalation**. Show the other party that they can only win if you win, too.
- Build a **'golden' bridge** between your positions. The other team should also be winners.

Put the words in bold in the text above into the following three categories.

agreement	deadlock	disagreement

AUDIO 15

1 Dyersville, France is hosting the International Student Summer Games this autumn. A British company, MQ Chemicals, has a subsidiary in the city and has agreed to sponsor the Games by covering half the costs. Sam Gilbert, a US television producer, calls the mayor, Maurice Bayle, to discuss their plans.

UNIT **6** Dealing with deadlock | **51**

Listen to the telephone conversation. Say whether the following sentences are true (✓) or false (✗).

1. The mayor is very polite to his caller. ☐
2. The mayor wants to stop the Games. ☐
3. The factory is important to the mayor and the city. ☐
4. The TV producer says the company has a new large order. ☐
5. The TV producer wants to close the factory. ☐
6. Mr Gilbert is polite to the mayor. ☐

EXPRESSIONS FOR DISAGREEING

Polite
I would prefer …
That is not how we see it.
Could you clarify that, please?
Could you explain that more fully, please?
I'm afraid we couldn't agree to that.

Less polite
You are wrong.
That is totally unacceptable.
No, that is out of the question.
No, I'm not interested.
I think you should explain.
I don't see the point.
Our experts say that …

Expressions to slow conversation down
Let me (just) make sure I understand what you are saying.
Let's go back and review the situation.
Why is that important to you?
How can we deal with/solve this problem?
Where does your information come from?

---

2 Listen to the conversation again. Write down the expressions you hear from the box above.

_____
_____
_____
_____
_____

3 The conversation between the mayor and Mr Gilbert contains the following expressions. Match them to their meanings.

Expression
1. ☐ don't have a clue
2. ☐ call the shots
3. ☐ go over your head
4. ☐ friends in high places
5. ☐ are not in the loop
6. ☐ be a non-starter

Meaning
a don't have all the information
b know important people
c don't understand
d will fail
e decide how things will be
f deal with your boss, not you

4 Repeat the conversation between the mayor and Mr Gilbert with a partner. This time use polite language. Use the transcript on pages 84–85.

5 Write a short, polite email from the mayor to the manager of MQ Chemicals. Inform the company about the conversation and explain the points made by Mr Gilbert.

From: Maurice Bayle [maurice.bayle@dyersville.fr] **To:** Simon Bennet [simon.bennet@mq-chemicals.uk]

Subject: International Student Summer Games

6 A meeting takes place in Simon Bennet's office. Listen to the conversation and take notes on the main points.

Problem:

Bennet's position:

Bayle's position:

Measures agreed:

UNIT **6** Dealing with deadlock | 53

> **EXPRESSIONS FOR DEALING WITH DISAGREEMENT OR DEADLOCK**
>
> **Making suggestions**
> Could the problem be solved by … ?
> Can you offer any alternatives?
>
> **Clarifying**
> Does that mean … ?
> How important is it for you that … ?
> What is the purpose of this policy?
>
> **Asking for suggestions**
> Can you offer us any other possibility?
> What would you suggest?
> What do you suggest I do?
>
> **Expressing partial agreement**
> I understand how you feel!
> I agree with you specifically on …
> Yes, you have a point there about …

7 Match the sentence beginnings (1–6) with the sentence endings (a–f).

1. Our **goal** is …
2. Does this **mean** …
3. It is our **opinion** that …
4. I am not in a **position** to do this …
5. You would have to …
6. The inspector thought …

a use the old **machines** too.
b a loss-making **subsidiary** must close.
c we had made good **progress**.
d to **complete** it by the end of August.
e the company will not **shut down** for the Games?
f because head office has already signed the **contract**.

8 Use the words in bold in exercise 7 to complete the sentences.

1. What do you _____? I do not understand.
2. I am very happy with your _____ in this company.
3. What is your _____ on a husband and wife working in the same department?
4. We have a _____ in China.
5. There is a _____ vacant in the finance department.
6. Please _____ the figures as soon as possible, as I must check them this week.
7. If you want to rent sewing _____, you must sign a five-year contract.
8. The shop _____ because there were not enough customers.

> **ADJOURNMENTS PAY OFF!**
>
> Inexperienced negotiators often avoid taking adjournments because they feel this might make them appear weak. Experienced negotiators, however, aren't afraid to call for a break. They frequently make effective use of them in order to:
>
> - consider a new point or proposal
> - reconsider a strategy or objective
> - get out of a circular argument
> - slow down the negotiation.
>
> When you wish to take an adjournment, follow these three steps:
> 1 Give a reason for the adjournment and state how much time is needed.
> 2 Summarize the current state of affairs before you go.
> 3 Withdraw to a private area.

ASKING QUESTIONS EFFECTIVELY

Asking questions has two purposes: getting information and building trust. In both cases, it is essential to be diplomatic. Therefore, ask **open** and **indirect questions**.

Open questions: An open question is created by using a question word like *how, when, why, which, who*, etc. A closed question, on the other hand, gives you a *yes/no* or *I don't know* answer. Open questions will give you much more information than closed questions. They will also help you get out of an impasse or stalemate. In an argument, each side will try to protect its interests. By using open questions, you show the other party you are interested in their concerns. And you can get some very helpful information, too!

Indirect questions: An indirect question in English is polite and, therefore, helps build trust. The indirect question reflects respect and politeness, e.g. *How did you arrive at that figure?* as compared to *Can you tell me how you arrived at that figure?*

If you want to build trust and get more information, ask open, indirect questions.

ASKING THE RIGHT QUESTIONS

Closed questions	vs.	Open questions
Is that important to you?		Why is that so important to you?
Who told you that?		Where does your information come from?
Who is the boss?		Do you have key managers in your company?
Will you pay our price?		What can you offer us?

Direct questions	vs.	Indirect questions
What is your budget for this project?		Can you give me an idea of your … ?
What do you mean … ?		Could you tell me … ?
What is your aim?		How do you think we can achieve this goal?

9 **Make the following questions open or indirect. Use the examples above to help you.**

1 Will you give us a 20% discount?

2 Do you supply other companies in Britain?

3 Does your company cause pollution?

4 Is the pollution decreasing?

5 Is your machinery out of date?

6 How can you prove no one will be harmed?

10 **Read the two letters and answer the questions on page 56.**

Healthwise Soft Drinks, 13, rue du centre, 66000 Perpignan

Monsieur Maurice Bayle
Mairie de Dyersville
55640 Dyersville

Dear Mr Mayor

As you know, we are sponsoring the ISS Games this summer. I was horrified to learn that the pollution level has reached an astronomical amount because of MQ Chemicals' outdated production methods. In addition, the air and water seem to be toxic. This pollution must stop by May for me to declare the area safe. Now it is not! Young people cannot come and be poisoned by the foul atmosphere caused by an outdated company.

The reputations of the city and our company would be ruined. I feel I speak from a position of strength. I can refuse to agree to let these Games take place. So strong demands must be made on this company. In addition, I have heard that production will double during the Games.

How can you allow this? I cannot. For this reason, I have no alternative but to issue an ultimatum. I will publish this letter nationally if you do not take action.

I insist we meet next week to discuss our combined strategy.

Regards
Dr Frank Simpson
Chief Medical Office

Maurice Bayle • Mairie de Dyersville • 55640 Dyersville

Dear Dr Simpson

I would be very happy to meet you to discuss this matter. I can quite understand your strong feelings and the specific points made in your email. I am sure that if I were in your position I would feel the same. Is next Friday at 10.00 am suitable?

Before our meeting, I would like some further information, as I am very interested in your position.

1. Is all the pollution definitely from the factory? Do you have the facts to back this up? Remember, there is a new motorway nearby.
2. We have drunk the local water for years. I will ask for new tests before the meeting. I hope that seems reasonable.

Regarding your demands to close the factory, I see this is logical from your point of view. However, many people losing their jobs would kill our town. I am sure that you will agree that this is an unacceptable solution. What do you feel we still need to do in order to resolve this issue?

Despite my many discussions with the company, they are not prepared to negotiate when threatened. In fact, they say they cannot discuss this matter at the moment. But if you are prepared to modify your demands, then we may be able to reach a compromise.

At present, I am in no position to issue an ultimatum. However, we need to discuss and resolve this matter at the meeting.

Yours
Maurice Bayle

The doctor is quite threatening and aggressive, while the mayor is trying to calm the situation.

1 Which expressions used by the doctor could be seen as threatening?
2 Which expressions does the mayor use to calm the situation?

PHRASES TO CALM A SITUATION AND RESOLVE PROBLEMS

Asking questions
Could you tell us why you feel like that?
How can we reach a compromise?
What do you think is a fair way to resolve … ?
Your position is very interesting. Can you tell me more?

Asking for or encouraging agreement with views
Do you agree with our position on … ?
Do you feel you can accept … ?
I hope you can see our point of view.
Let me explain our position!

Expressing agreement
I know exactly what you mean.
I believe that is correct.
That seems reasonable.
If I were in your position, I would also …

Phrases that can appear threatening
demand
negotiate under duress
issue an ultimatum
be in a position of strength

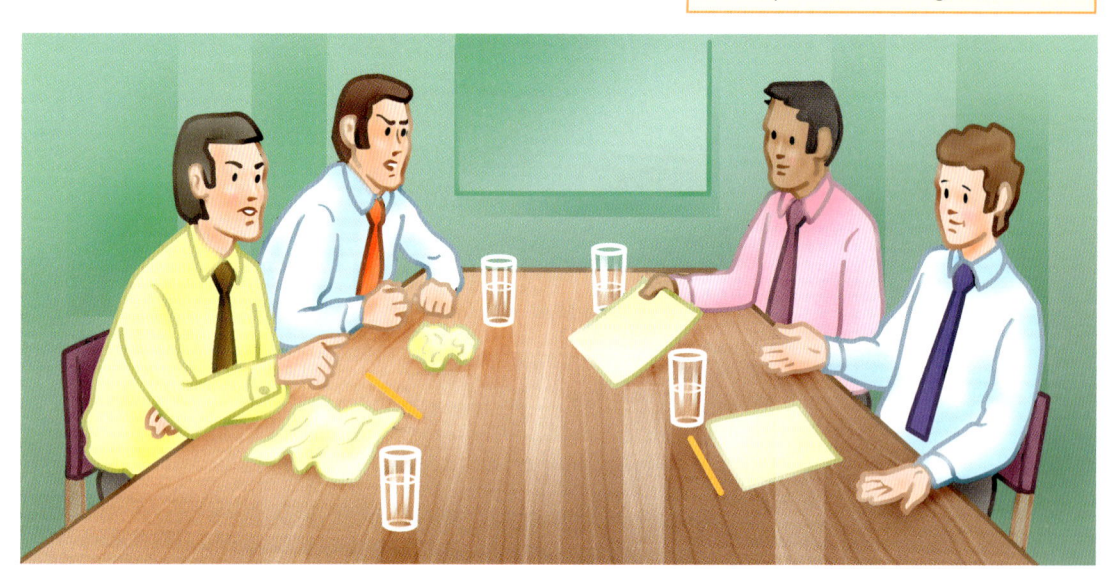

YOUR BODY TALKS

A good impression is often the result of the right amount of eye contact and personal space with respect to the other party.

Studies show the average amount of **eye contact** with North Americans and Western Europeans should be about a third of the time. In general, Latin Americans and Southern Europeans prefer more eye contact, whereas African Americans prefer less.

Personal space is also another important factor. It is often divided into three zones.
- The *intimate* zone (< 45 cm) is reserved for partners, children, and close family members.
- The *personal* zone (45 cm – 1.3 m) is for friends and acquaintances.
- The *social* zone (1.3 – 3 m) is for formal interaction.

As a rule, if eye contact is too little or if you stand too far away, this may imply that you feel shy, guilty, or bored. If there is too much eye contact or you stand too close, then you may be considered rude, hostile, or challenging.

UNIT **6** Dealing with deadlock | 57

11 In this unit there were many concerns about pollution issues. Use Mr Bennet's notes to write a memo explaining the problems to his head office in Britain.

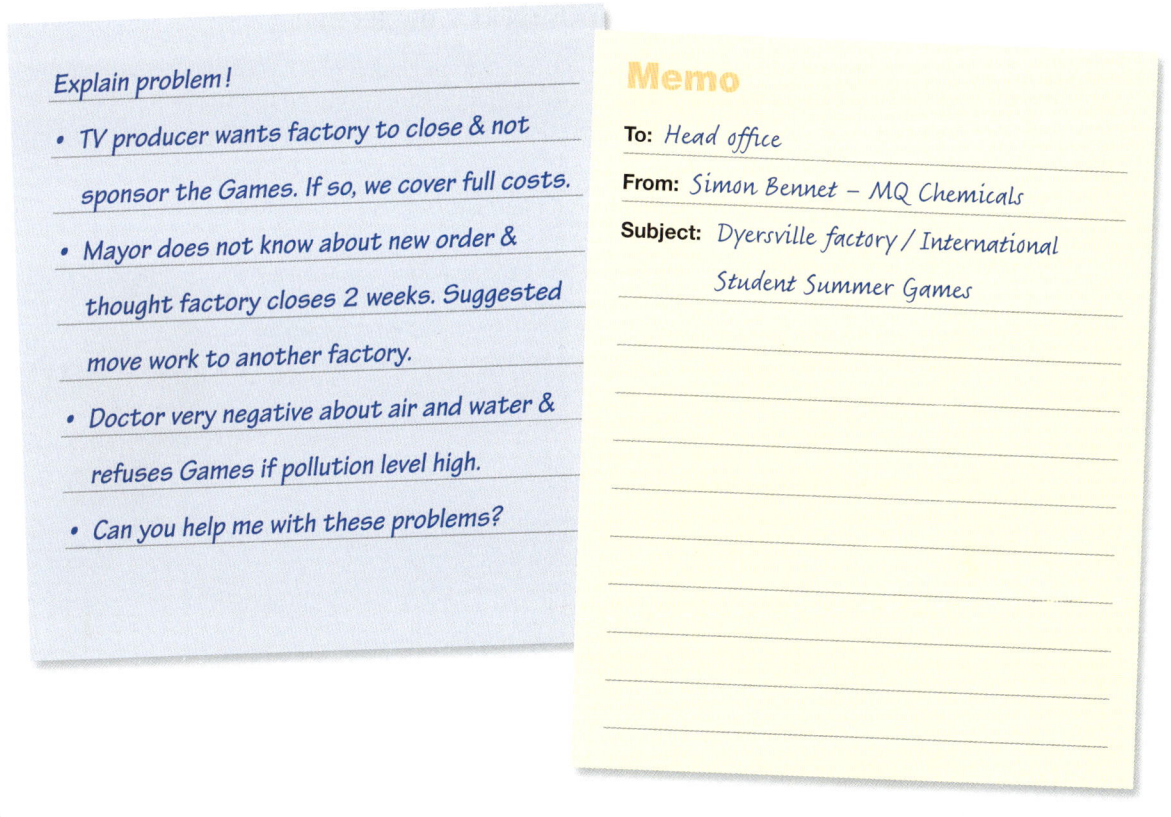

Explain problem!
- *TV producer wants factory to close & not sponsor the Games. If so, we cover full costs.*
- *Mayor does not know about new order & thought factory closes 2 weeks. Suggested move work to another factory.*
- *Doctor very negative about air and water & refuses Games if pollution level high.*
- *Can you help me with these problems?*

Memo

To: Head office
From: Simon Bennet – MQ Chemicals
Subject: Dyersville factory / International Student Summer Games

12 The mayor is holding a meeting in the city hall. Just before the meeting he has a short telephone conversation with Simon Bennet. Listen to the conversation and decide what you think the solution could be.

> **BUILDING THE GOLDEN BRIDGE**
> I got this idea from something you said earlier …
> This occurred to me as a follow-up to our previous discussion.
> Which interests of yours does this still not satisfy?
> Is there any way we can make this offer better for you?

13 A builder wants to develop a property for industrial use. He meets a representative of the local residents' association, who has many objections to the development.

PARTNER FILES Partner A File 6, p. 71
Partner B File 6, p. 73

OUTPUT

Read the article.

Give them what they want, but on your terms!

At the beginning of a negotiation, a lot of positioning takes place as each party presents its views. As the negotiation progresses, trust is built up bit by bit and information begins to be shared between the parties. This signals the real heart of the negotiation.

In order to give them what they want, but on your terms, you need to link issues!
Here are some comments by experienced negotiators about linking issues:

Jo Greendown, CEO: When negotiating one issue at a time, negotiators will generally agree on the easy ones first and set aside the more difficult ones until the end, when they often have very little to trade off. Multiple-issue offers link outcomes. However, this means you have to quickly move from asking questions to consolidating the information into an offer.

Boris Mayr, CFO: Keep in mind that making multiple-issue offers will give you even more information. As a result, this generates many more options for mutual gain and lets you get the most out of the deal.

Susanne Schmidt, MBA, Logistics Manager: You need to keep the big picture in mind. A good HIT list will help you. Think the way your opponent thinks! You need to put yourself in their shoes and focus on their benefits.

Gregory Lau, Sales & Marketing Director: Take a break! An adjournment will help you collect your thoughts, and, as a team, confirm your strategy. This allows you to be more flexible with your approach and helps you recognize different alternatives. You are also less likely to overlook additional options.

Dr. Laura Going, CIO: Multiple-issue offers minimize the need to build up trust because they don't force parties to reveal specific goals and priorities on individual issues. But they also avoid distrust, since negotiators rarely make multiple-issues offers that they aren't willing to agree to at the end of the day.

OVER TO YOU

- Do you agree with the statements above? Why, or why not?
- Discuss the situation in the partner file again. This time, find an approach where you can link multiple issues together.
- Look at a negotiation you were involved with in the past. If you did it again, how could you give them what they want, but on your terms?

7 Agreement

STARTER We need a volunteer! The rest of the class has to leave the room. Choose a topic below and summarize it. Call in a student (A) and present your summary. Now call in another student (B) and ask student A to summarize what they heard for student B. Have each student enter the classroom one by one. The last student presents the final summary to the whole class.

- a film
- a book
- a current event
- your last holiday

Discuss.

1. How much is left of the original story after the last person has told it?
2. Did the main points get through to the end?
3. What made summarizing difficult? What was helpful?

AUDIO 18

1 Mr Fisher and his partners are financing a housing project. During the last few weeks they have been negotiating the contract. Now he is meeting with a lawyer, Mr Clark, in order to finalize the agreement. Listen to the dialogue and say whether the following statements are true (✔) or false (✗).

1. Mr Fisher and his partners want to pay for all the kitchens and garden sheds.
2. The agent agrees to include all the kitchens and garden sheds in the purchase price.
3. Mr Fisher wants to sign the contract in two weeks.
4. Mr Clark and his client are unhappy with the agreement so far.
5. Mr Fisher's partners are unable to attend the meeting.

MOVING NEGOTIATIONS ALONG

Describing current/future situations
Fortunately, …
Unfortunately, we haven't been able to …
We are very satisfied/dissatisfied …
In future we hope to …
Hopefully, we will be able to …
By the time we …

Expressing agreement
I/We can only agree with you there.
I/We have to admit that you are right.
I am/We are willing to work with that.
That is also our concern/point of view/goal.
By mutual agreement we have decided to …
It's a deal!

Conveying commitment
I am/We are sure we can find a solution to …
I am/We are committed to finding a solution.
I/We have no doubt that …
We hope to be able to come to an agreement.
We are looking forward to a successful business relationship.

Stating progress made or current status
I believe we have made some good progress.
This is certainly a step towards …
Fine, but it seems we still need to discuss …
In order to achieve our objectives, we still …

2 Look at the Useful Language box above. Underline all the expressions you heard in the dialogue.

3 Complete the sentences with the words below. An example has been done for you.

Example: By the time / have / information / sign / contract.

By the time *we have this information, we will be able to sign the contract.*

1 This contract / result / our / mutual agreement.

_____

2 This is certainly a step towards / settlement / contract.

_____

3 I have no doubt / seller / open / last-minute / change.

_____

4 Hopefully, we will / be able / provide / details / ten days.

_____

5 It seems we still need to discuss / price / order / achieve / objectives.

_____

6 We are very satisfied / way / talks / going.

_____

UNIT 7   Agreement | 61

4 Answer the following questions by choosing expressions from the Useful Phrases on page 60. Complete the sentences with the content from the listening in 1 where necessary.

1   Do you think it is possible to resolve the situation?
    _____

2   That was a successful afternoon, wasn't it?
    _____

3   How do you feel about our new proposal?
    _____

4   Do you think your client will agree?
    _____

5   Do you have any news from your client?
    _____

6   How do you feel about the meeting so far?
    _____

DIRTY TRICKS

Although negotiators generally consider themselves to be very logical, many of their decisions are made without thinking them through! Sometimes tactics are used to make negotiators uncomfortable and force quick, gut reactions. Here are some common tactics:

- Demand immediate responses.
- Don't allow breaks or time to rest.
- Make personal negative comments.
- Always refer back to concessions already made.
- Explain that the bosses just won't agree.
- Add a demand to every concession made.

Don't let yourself be pressurized by these tactics. Remain calm and take your time to consider the implications before you respond.

AUDIO 19

5 Mr Fisher discusses the details with Mr Clark. Listen and answer the following questions.

1   When will Mr Fisher take possession of the houses?
2   Did Mr Fisher agree to the purchase price of 2.75 million?
3   Will the meeting continue at 4.30 p.m.?

READING BETWEEN THE LINES

According to research done by Edward T. Hall, a 'yes' in Japanese ('hai') may not have the same meaning as 'yes' in English. Communication has many dimensions and information is often embedded between the words, rather than directly on the surface. Non-Western cultures (e.g. Japanese, Russian, and Arab cultures) generally use indirect communication more often than Western cultures (e.g. Britain, the US, and Switzerland). Indirect communication requires interpreting words together with their social context. Understand the culture and you'll more fully understand a person's message and intentions. Therefore, listen carefully, observe intensely, and don't make assumptions.

BRINGING NEGOTIATIONS TO A HEAD

Guaranteeing
I/We guarantee you that …
I/We can assure you that …
I/We will do my/our best to …

Discussing follow-up documentation
Shall we put this into a written proposal?
I think we will need a detailed summary of this.
Let's draft a contract based on these points!

Summarizing
(Just) to summarize …
So far we have established …
Let me just repeat, if I may.
This is where we stand.
I would like to summarize as follows …
I/We think/believe we all agree here that …
We have certainly covered a lot of ground today!

6 Look at the following statements. Which category do they belong in: A, B, or C?

A Discussing follow-up documentation
B Guaranteeing
C Summarizing

1. I will do my best to ensure the contract is signed today.
2. This is where we stand at the moment.
3. Shall we put this into a written proposal?
4. Let me just repeat the last two statements, if I may.
5. We assure you that the quality will not change.
6. We have certainly covered a lot of ground today!
7. Let's draft a final outline based on these points!

UNIT 7   Agreement | 63

7 Rewrite the statements using the Useful Phrases on page 62.

1 I guess we need an itemized list of this part of the contract.
   _____

2 I can assure you that the house will be available in July.
   _____

3 OK, this is how it is at the moment.
   _____

4 We have really done a lot of work today.
   _____

5 We can now set up the contract with these details.
   _____

6 Can I just recap on these points?
   _____

> **DON'T MISS THE CLOSE!**
>
> It is surprising how often negotiators miss the close. Many are afraid to end the negotiations because they fear they may have missed or forgotten something. The other side often misinterprets this fear as a delay tactic and believes that the first party is uninterested or wants even more. They then become confused and defensive and the agreement begins to fall apart.
>
> Closing is a matter of instinct as well as common sense. Look for the non-verbal signals and listen for the verbal ones. Keep your goal in mind. If you've reached it, then make the deal!

AUDIO 20

8 It is 4.30 p.m. and Mr Clark and Mr Fisher meet again in order to sign the contract as discussed that morning. Listen to their conversation. Then fill in the gaps with the words from the box.

> contract signifies • drawn up • finalized • for having us • guarantee • implement
> • look at the changes • signature • you can go

1 No problem, Mr Clark. We both know that this was necessary. Have you _____ the contract?

2 No, not really. I only want to _____ we have discussed today and then I will sign the document. Oh, has your client signed it already?

3 Yes, and if you turn to the last page, his _____ is right … there.

4 Congratulations, Mr Fisher! This _____ the successful conclusion of a lot of hard work over the past couple of weeks.

5 When we have _____ the contract, we will submit it to the relevant authorities.

6 Hmm, I know this may sound a bit impatient, but we would be grateful if you could _____ this by the end of the week.

7 Of course. Then we can _____ access to the project site any time we would like, can't we?

8 Yes, you can. In fact, _____ next Monday. … Well, it has been a pleasure.

9 Yes, it has. I also speak for my partners when I say thank you _____.

9 **Listen to the conversation again. Put the phrases you hear which are used to express deadlines and close discussions in the table below.**

Expressing deadlines	Closing discussions
… implement this by …	… thank you for having us

BRINGING NEGOTIATIONS TO A CLOSE

Expressing deadlines
We should come to a decision within/by …
You will be hearing from us by …
The closing date for … is …
I/We would be grateful if you could implement this by …

Closing discussion
Thank you for coming.
Thank you for having us.
Thank you for a fruitful discussion/productive meeting.
I/We had hoped/expected to get a lot out of this meeting.
I am/We are very much looking forward to …
We would certainly like to intensify …

10 Write five sentences expressing deadlines with the words below.

date		Monday		complete
deadline		Friday		documents
decision	by	9th		exchange
finish	for	21st	in order to	finalize agreement
hear	of	4.30 p.m.	to	obtain information
implement	within	3 weeks		paperwork
set		4 days		problem
time limit		5 months		sort/solve

1 _____
2 _____
3 _____
4 _____
5 _____

11 Look at two negotiation scenarios. Choose one of the scenarios and close the negotiation.

Scenario 1
– close a major deal
– establish new partnership
– have high expectations at the start

Scenario 2
– solve a problem
– increase business activity
– look round the production facility

Write down possible sentences and practise them with a partner.

_____
_____
_____
_____
_____

12 Read the cover letter sent by Mr Clark to Mr Fisher.

Clark & Partners, Law Firm
---

13 June 2010

Subject: Holland Drive development

Dear Mr Fisher

As discussed this week I am contacting you with respect to the above.

Attached you will find a copy of the contract for your records. **As you will see**, my clients have signed the contract. In addition, all the relevant authorities have given their approval. This means that you have as of this weekend direct access to the property.

We assume that you will carry out the bank transfer by the end of the month. **Please note** that bank details can be found on the first page of the contract.

If you require any additional information, **please do not hesitate to** contact us. Should you be interested in purchasing additional property, **please feel free to** inform us at your convenience. We **look forward** to dealing with you in future.

Best regards

Kenneth Clark

Now fill in the gaps in the sentences below with the words in bold.

1 _____ that you will discuss this with your shareholders and then get back to us.

2 If you require additional material on the project, _____ inform us.

3 _____ in our last meeting, we are sending you a formal confirmation of our position on the matter.

4 Should you require further details on aspects of the offer, _____ contact us at your convenience.

5 _____, we have made the changes we agreed on.

6 We _____ to working with you on this project in future.

7 _____ that we can maintain our offer only until the end of next month.

8 _____ you will find a counterproposal for the project.

13 A sportswear supplier and a sportswear retailer have been negotiating the supply of running equipment. Today they want to finalize the agreement.

PARTNER FILES Partner A File 7, p. 71
Partner B File 7, p. 73

OUTPUT

Read the following article from an online newsletter.

A negotiation is successful when …

Proof that negotiations have been successful is both subjective and objective. There are certainly goals that have to be reached. But success cannot only be measured in these terms. Here are some other important aspects to keep in mind:

Success is when both parties …

- **feel that they have achieved success**. The sense of accomplishment is very important to the personal ego of all parties involved. Feeling that we have reached the goal we set out for ourselves is important and cannot be underestimated. Recognize this for the other party, too!
- **feel appreciated**. When we feel that the other party appreciated our interests and was interested in us, this gives us pleasure. Lack of appreciation makes us hesitate and unwilling to continue a working relationship.
- **feel the other side was fair**. There is nothing worse than closing a deal, only to find out afterwards that the other side took advantage of you. The concept of fairness is common to us all and the basis upon which trust is built. There is no trust without fairness.
- **feel that professional and objective standards have been applied**. In a successful negotiation, the agreement needs to be based on a measurement independent of both parties. In other words, all parties involved feel that acceptable and objective criteria or standards have been used.
- **feel the other side will keep the agreement**. It is very disappointing when the other party comes back a few days later and nullifies the agreement. A lot of hard work goes into a negotiation. Finding out it was for nothing will destroy any reputation and goodwill that was built up. It also leaves a sour aftertaste.
- **would deal with each other again**. A quick 'acid test' before the deal is closed is whether you would deal with the other party again in the future. This reflects your 'gut feeling'. Listen to it!

OVER TO YOU

- Do you agree with the points mentioned in the online newsletter? Why, or why not?
- Think about a negotiation you have been in. Was it successful according to the above criteria?
- How important is the feeling of success for you personally? Should it influence your goal?

Test yourself!

See how much vocabulary you have learned. Use the clues to complete the crossword puzzle.

Across
- 3 A situation in which neither party can win; also used in chess.
- 5 An angry disagreement between parties.
- 6 The official record of a meeting.
- 8 A booking for a hotel or flight.
- 11 A list of topics or points to be discussed at a meeting.
- 12 A place to hold a meeting.
- 15 A situation in which neither party sees a possible next step.
- 19 A timetable or programme.
- 20 Your position on a subject.
- 22 Money paid by the state or a company when you no longer work.
- 23 A situation in which both parties have achieved their objectives.
- 25 A position in which someone is neither for nor against something.
- 26 A firm request.
- 27 A first proposal.
- 28 A discussion between parties who would like to reach an agreement.

Down
- 1 Another word for a goal.
- 2 Companies owned or controlled by another company.
- 4 An additional possibility beyond the present one.
- 6 The term used to say that both parties approve of the decision.
- 7 A person who offers products on the market for a price.
- 9 To officially inform someone about something.
- 10 An item in your proposal which you are prepared to exchange for something you want more.
- 13 The date by which an action must take place.
- 14 Another word for an offer in a negotiation.
- 16 An alternative you might choose.
- 17 A business agreement often confirmed by a handshake.
- 18 An alternative provided in response to an offer.
- 21 A document which is signed when a deal is finalized.
- 24 An article or object on a list.

Test yourself! | **69**

Partner A — Partner files

UNIT 1, Exercise 10 — File 1

Take a look at your list of 'H's' in exercise 7. Then study the information in the partner file. Compare your list with the points below. Note all possible 'H's'. Get any missing information from your partner and set your 'H's'.

Site	Location	Size	Rent/Purchase	Additional Information	Price
Greenfield	Shanghai	2,000 m²	10-year lease	no buildings, needs planning permission	€ 10,000 p.a.
Brownfield	Kowloon	1,500 m²	purchase only	4 factory buildings unused for 5 years, 1 new office block, partly occupied	purchase price to be agreed
Old Railway	Beijing	2,500 m²	rent or purchase	all buildings need to be removed, good access to motorway	€ 15,000 p.a. lease purchase price to be agreed
New Industrial Park	Shanghai	_____ m²	10-year lease	2 factories, 1 office block, newly built	€ _____ p.a.
Kowloon Park	Kowloon	1,500 m²	purchase only	4 factory buildings, 2 of which occupied, 1 office block, needs refurbishing	purchase price to be agreed
Temple Park	_____	2,600 m²	_____	to be developed, planning permission available, can be bought after lease is up	€ 8,500 p.a.

Now write sentences a) stating your 'H's' and b) providing an explanation for them.

UNIT 2, Exercise 10 — File 2

You are a British architect. You have to contact partners in different companies and countries, and hope to get them all to London for a meeting on the same day. You want to discuss proposals with them to modernize your company's working practices and to make some decisions.

Arrange a meeting lasting half a day with the French salesperson who is the first person on your list.

This is your schedule for the week.

Monday	7.30–12.30	sales meeting
Tuesday	8.00–9.30	English lesson
	12.30–1.30	lunch with directors
	3.30	dentist
Wednesday	Morning	Oxford
	Afternoon	drive back to London
Thursday		English Public Holiday
Friday		Take the day off, if possible!

UNIT 3, Exercise 16 — File 3

You are a buyer for a large department store and you would like to discuss the following points:

- You want to reduce prices, but need a guarantee on quality.
- A meeting is urgent. Ideally, it must be before the end of the month.
- You would also like to add in a final point.
- Deliveries must be on time in future.
- You want to introduce your assistant, who will be taking over womenswear next year.
- Some of the designs in the catalogue are outdated.

Set the agenda with your partner. At the meeting, introduce your colleagues to your partner.

UNIT 4, Exercise 16 — File 4

You are the purchasing manager of the company. You need to buy a fleet of new cars for the sales representatives. You have clear ideas as to the features the cars should have and the price you would like to pay.

These are your notes:

- Car: X-type with 5 doors
- Colour: black metallic at no extra charge
- Engine: diesel
- Summer and winter tyres/wheels
- Air conditioning
- Price: min €12,000 up to a max of €13,000

Tell the class whether a deal has been reached! If so, what were the terms?

UNIT 5, Exercise 14 — File 5

You represent an employers' association, which has made the following offer:
a pay increase of 3% and an increase in working hours by one hour.

At the end of the first round of negotiations, both you and your partner have agreed to take a break to think about the following compromise:
4% and a half-hour increase in working hours.
Nevertheless, there are still other benefits that could help you come to a good compromise:

- early retirement scheme
- job guarantees for employees over 50
- sabbatical year
- further training programme paid for by company for employees longer than three years on board
- contribution to pension scheme financed by company raised by 3%
- luncheon vouchers
- contribution towards transportation cost to company.

Discuss these alternatives and try and come up with a win–win solution. Use phrases which express, clarify, and respond to proposals as well as suggest solutions.

UNIT 6, Exercise 13 — File 6

You are the builder. Your project has many advantages:

- The building site will provide jobs.
- Companies will open in the buildings, which will help lower the unemployment rate.
- The factory units will be modern and ecologically friendly.
- Many local people want the old buildings pulled down because they are dangerous.

A survey of the local residents shows that most people are in favour of the project. From your point of view, the results of the survey are good. Use the survey to help solve the problem.

However, you are under pressure because you have already bought the land and must get permission to build soon.

Stay polite if your partner tries to attack your points.

UNIT 7, Exercise 13 — File 7

You are a sportswear supplier and have been negotiating with a new client for the supply of running equipment.

Now you are meeting with your new customer to finalize the agreement. Summarize the information you have agreed on, set up an action plan, and close the negotiation.

Item(s)	Quantity p.a.	Quality	Price
Running shoes high	500 pcs.	leather	€49
Running shoes mid	300 pcs.	leather/cloth	€35
Running shoes low	450 pcs.	suede leather	€30
Running shorts black	500 pcs.	nylon/cotton	€15
Running shorts white	500 pcs	pure cotton	€14
Running top black	1,000 pcs.	mixed fibres	€15
Running top white	750 pcs.	pure cotton	€14

Partner B — Partner files

UNIT 1, Exercise 10 — File 1

Take a look at your list of 'H's' in exercise 7. Then study the information in the partner file. Compare your list with the points below. Note all possible 'H's'. Get any missing information from your partner and set your 'H's'.

Site	Location	Size	Rent/Purchase	Additional Information	Price
Greenfield	_____	2,000 m²	10-year lease	no buildings, needs planning permission	€ 10,000 p.a.
Brownfield	Kowloon	1,500 m²	_____	4 factory buildings unused for 5 years, 1 new office block, partly occupied	_____
Old Railway	Beijing	_____ m²	rent or purchase	all buildings need to be removed, good access to motorway	€ 15,000 p.a. lease purchase price to be agreed
New Industrial Park	Shanghai	2,250 m²	10-year lease	2 factories, 1 office block, newly built	€ 20,000 p.a.
Kowloon Park	Kowloon	1,500 m²	purchase only	4 factory buildings, 2 of which occupied, 1 office block, needs refurbishing	purchase price to be agreed
Temple Park	Beijing	2,600 m²	5-year lease	to be developed, planning permission available, can be bought after lease is up	€ 8,500 p.a.

Now write sentences a) stating your 'H's' and b) providing an explanation for them.

UNIT 2, Exercise 10 — File 2

You are a French salesperson representing a French company selling new software for designing houses. Your partner, a British architect, has invited you to come to London for a meeting. Your company thinks the British company could become an important business partner. You want to go to London to discuss your products.

Arrange a meeting. Can you change some arrangements?

Here is your schedule for the week.

Monday	7.30–12.30	free
	Afternoon	product presentation meeting
Tuesday	9.00–12.00	meeting with advertising company
	Afternoon	free
Wednesday	Morning	meeting with managing director
	Afternoon	on the road with sales team
Thursday		all day free
Friday	Morning	free
	Afternoon	pick up family from airport

UNIT 3, Exercise 16 — File 3

You sell ladies' and children's fashion and you would like to discuss the following points:

- You are bringing your new boss with you to deal with complaints from last year.
- You sell an excellent quality product, which is reflected in the price.
- You cannot agree to anything, as your CEO is on holiday until next month.
- You would like more flexibility on deliveries.
- You have an excellent new designer for the children's range.

Set the agenda with your partner. At the meeting, introduce your colleagues to your partner.

Partner files | **73**

UNIT 4, Exercise 16 — File 4

You are the owner of a car dealership. You are talking to a potential customer and hope to make a sale and a good profit.

You base your discussions on the following information:

- Car: X-type with 3 or 5 doors
- Colour: black, red, blue, and silver. Metallic paint at extra charge of €150
- Winter tyres/wheels cost €250, but can be given free – if customer accepts price without discount
- Air conditioning: €250 can be offered with a 50% discount – if ordered by the end of the week
- One free inspection per year on offer – if customer needs to be persuaded
- Price: diesel engine €14,500, petrol engine €13,500 (a max of 10% discount available on both)

Tell the class whether a deal has been reached! If so, what were the terms?

UNIT 5, Exercise 14 — File 5

You represent a trade union which has made the following demands:
a pay increase of 6% and no increase in hours!

At the end of the first round of negotiations, both you and your partner have agreed to take a break and think about the following compromise:
4% and a half-hour increase in working hours.

Nevertheless, there are still other benefits that could help you come to a good compromise:

- early retirement scheme
- job guarantees for employees over 50
- sabbatical year
- further training programme paid for by company for employees longer than three years on board
- contribution to pension scheme financed by company raised by 3%
- luncheon vouchers
- contribution towards transportation cost to company.

Discuss these alternatives and try and come up with a win–win solution. Use phrases which express, clarify, and respond to proposals as well as suggest solutions.

UNIT 6, Exercise 13 — File 6

You represent the local residents' association. You have just moved to this quiet town and are afraid of the following:

- The town will expand too quickly.
- The buildings will increase traffic.
- All factories are dirty and noisy.
- The town will lose its character.

Make sure the builder understands that your points are strong ones! Be firm! They must prove that the town will benefit and that the environment is safe.

You have a strong opinion and you use colourful expressions. At times you might even be a bit impolite.

UNIT 7, Exercise 13 — File 7

You are a sportswear retailer and have been negotiating with a new supplier for the supply of running equipment. This is the meeting in which you hope to finalize the agreement, set up an action plan, and close the negotiation.

Your notes were done in pencil, so some of the information is hard to read. Unfortunately, you left the printed copy in the office. You also have one point which you would like to change.

Item(s)	Quantity p.a.	Quality	Price
Running shoes high	500 pcs.	leather	€49
Running shoes mid	300 pcs.	leather/cloth	€35
Running shoes low	450 pcs.	suede leather	€30
~~	500 pcs.	~~~~ cotton	€15
Running shorts white	500 pcs	pure cotton	€14
Running top black	1,000 pcs.	mixed fibres	€15*
Running top white	750 pcs.	pure cotton	€14

* need to change the quality to pure cotton because the mix of fibres is not going to sell well

Answer key

UNIT 1

page 6

1
1. On June 24th at 10.30 a.m.
2. Tasha, Karin, Frank, and Mirja
3. To negotiate a master agreement
4. A quality report
5. Ten working days

page 7

2 **To ask for information (underlined expressions):**
Please let me know (2 x)   Can you check
Could you please do   let me know
I require

To plan a meeting (circled expressions):
to schedule a meeting
set up an agenda
find a date
I propose we meet on
we have to talk about
Would you please join us

3
1. negotiation
2. proposal
3. to arrange
4. discussion
5. to prepare
6. to calculate
7. delivery
8. to pay
9. quotation
10. to specify
11. production
12. transportation
13. chairperson/chair
14. to inform
15. to produce
16. meeting

page 8

4 Possible answers:
- Have you got a moment?
- Can I ask you a favour? Can you finish off the calculation by 9 o'clock, please?
- Can you help me with the proposal, please?
- Can you find out the price for me?
- Where is the yellow folder? I need it.
- Do you have any more details on the colours available?
- Who is in charge of the production department?
- Do you know the address of the delivery company?
- Can you tell me what the word 'haggling' means?

page 9

5
1. F – It is on June 24th.
2. F – She asked him for details from a report. The minute-taker has not been decided.
3. F – The price is not too bad.
4. F – They are not as expected.
5. F – She has to look at the figures again.
6. T
7. T

page 10

6 Possible answers:
- The right price for the goods because price is a critical factor.
- Short delivery times because it ensures continuous production in one's own factory and allows for just-in-time delivery.
- Product quality because that avoids problems with the end customer.
- Discounts on large quantities because it gives Tasha more scope for profit with her own customers.
- Good relationship with Jackson's so that she will not have to look for new business partners.
- Flexibility in case of a rush on certain products.

7 Possible answers:
- We want easy access to transport routes such as motorways and ports.
- We would like a good price for the land.
- This is because suppliers are situated close by.
- Future developments complement our products and our plans.
- The reason is that it is big enough for possible future expansion.
- Good quality buildings that give customers a good impression are essential.
- We need to buy land.
- We must lease land for a long period.

page 11

8
1. 1905
2. Jackson
3. grandson
4. Development
5. sales
6. David
7. Hallam
8. Asia
9. England
10. fall, reduction or drop
11. lost
12. reduce
13. customers
14. that he wants to develop the Asian market

page 12

9 Possible answers:

For	Against
Family-owned business, continuity	Too traditional and maybe old-fashioned
High technical standard	Financial problems
Based in England	Might move production to China or import
Joint venture with Chinese partner	Will quality remain the same?
New partner has good reputation	Possibly longer delivery times

UNIT 2

page 14

1 Possible answers:
economies of scale, branch closures, customer complaints, publicity, corporate identity

page 16

3
1. F – She is happy for them to appoint the chairperson.
2. F – She wants the meeting to be held on 18th February.

3 T
4 F – She thinks the marketing department should be in Latvia.
5 T
6 F – She wants to close as few British branches as possible.
7 T

4
1 Johannes DaVita
2 Marketing
3 Public
4 Customer
5 Branch
6 Corporate
7 combining

page 17

5a Underlined phrases:
We must
I think we will have to agree to
Johannes and I think it is important
I am willing to accept
Perhaps we could trade this idea against
I would also like to keep our name
I refuse to accept
This might mean that

5b

Essential (H)	Important (I)	Exchangeable points (T)
Public Relations Consultant	Call centres and computer centres close	Close corporate centre
Customers notified in advance	Some British branches open	Son combines computer systems
Marketing staff redundancies	Keep name	British advertising expert

6 AGENDA
1 Apologies for absence
2 Appointment of Public Relations Consultant
3 Marketing Department
4 Notification of customers
5 Corporate centres
6 Branch closures
7 Advertising
8 Corporate image and branding
9 Computers
10 Call centres
11 AOB
12 Date of next meeting

page 19

7
1 December 19th
2 February 11th in London
3 No, they have asked if there are any.
4 Her reason is that no agenda had been received.
5 January 27th

page 20

8 Meeting details
Date: February 18th
Time: 9.00 a.m.
Place: Oracle Bank Board Room

UNIT 3

page 23

2
1 No
2 Yes
3 No
4 Don't know
5 Don't know
6 Don't know

page 24

3
1 This is to confirm the date of the next meeting.
2 Following our telephone conversation there are still a few open points for the agenda.
3 Attached you will find a summary of the current financial status of the company.
4 I look forward to meeting you and discussing the topic with you.

page 25

4 caller – Mark Taylor
company – Bookmark PLC
comments – Agenda
           Added pricing before advertising
           Other arrangements agreed
contact – Mark

5 … have received the revised agenda
… on this basis
… has reminded us that …
I look forward to meeting you.

6

at	in	on
2.30 p.m.	January	… time
4.40 p.m.	… time	Monday
three o'clock	the morning	
the weekend	the afternoon	
lunchtime	2010	

7
1 We will meet **on** Wednesday **at** 5.00 p.m.
2 I am going to see my boss **on** an important matter.
3 I do not like writing emails **at** night. In general I prefer working **in** the morning.
4 Where shall we go **at** lunchtime **on** Monday?
5 If you cannot be **on** time, please give me a call.
6 The meeting will be held **at** our headquarters **in** my office **on** Tuesday afternoon.

page 26

9
1 Bookmark's main goals are the following: a) get a quick agreement, b) take on their better quality titles, c) have Books to Go organize a joint website and contribute to the costs, and d) access Books to Go's catalogue of self-help and business development books.
2 Books to Go's main objectives are to a) get some money from Bookmark's for the website, b) get Books to Go's books into Bookmark's market, and c) get a good deal on the list of non-fiction titles.
3 No
4 Bookmark
5 Books to Go

10 1e B   2d BTG   3a BTG   4c B   5b B

page 27

11
1 He is a website expert.
2 He is Operations Director.
3 He wants to explain how long he has been in the Internet business.
4 Yes.

12 May I introduce … He is …
How do you do?
Very pleased to meet you.
It is a pleasure to meet you.

page 28

14 1 put up
2 come up with
3 go along with
4 fall in with
5 look forward to

15 1 e 2 c 3 d 4 b 5 a

UNIT 4

page 31

1 1 One shipment for all the goods
2 Production time of 15 working days and four days for transportation   P
3 Pick-up by customer
4 Part-shipment   P
5 Delivery by air freight
6 Delivery of three (not four) shipments   CP
7 Working longer hours   CP
8 Production time of 15 working days and two days for transportation

2 See transcript on page 82.

3 1 F 2 T 3 F 4 T 5 T 6 T

page 32

4 Possible answers:
1 · How do you feel about delivery within ten working days?
· Is it alright with you if we deliver within ten working days?
2 · I propose working two shifts instead of three shifts.
· You suggested working in two shifts instead of three shifts. This is correct, isn't it?
3 · Would delivery in part-shipments at seven-day intervals be an alternative?
· Can you tell me how you would arrange delivery at seven-day intervals?
4 · We suggest delivering larger amounts in fewer shipments. What is your opinion?
· How do you feel about delivery in larger amounts and fewer shipments?
5 · Can you imagine a delivery of one shipment?
· Can you tell me how you deliver in one shipment?

5 Possible answers:
· I suggest using a different forwarder.
· How about a shorter delivery time?
· Can you tell me how much shorter the delivery time would be?
· Would regular shipments every six weeks be an alternative?
· Can you tell me how you will transport the goods?

page 33

6 1 Could you imagine increasing the order amount by 10%?
2 How do you feel about 500 pieces per order?
3 Can you tell me how the goods are stored?
4 How about transport by rail instead of by truck?
5 Is it alright with you if we load in a container?
6 Would sea freight be an alternative?
7 What is your opinion on a part-shipment?

page 33–34

7 1 talked about
2 unable to accept
3 not going
4 not an option
5 Maybe
6 you can do
7 Maybe we can
8 we cannot
9 that means no

page 34

8 1 expectation
2 imagine
3 unfortunately
4 propose
5 proposal
6 doubtful
7 possible
8 alternative
9 unlikely
10 alternative
11 possibility
12 opinion
13 question
14 expect

page 35

9

P	D	O	U	B	T	F	U	L	I	K	E	L	Y	Z
O	I	D	I	F	L	I	P	N	P	Y	T	H	E	N
S	S	M	M	O	T	W	R	U	L	E	O	U	T	O
S	T	I	A	D	E	P	O	S	S	I	B	L	E	T
I	I	D	G	G	U	M	P	L	O	N	K	S	S	E
B	N	C	I	N	I	P	O	P	E	N	T	E	N	F
I	C	A	N	I	T	N	S	V	Q	U	A	W	L	A
L	T	M	A	Y	E	N	E	X	P	E	C	T	O	Y
I	A	L	T	E	R	N	A	T	I	V	E	N	T	A
T	M	P	I	B	O	P	I	N	I	O	N	O	U	N
Y	P	R	O	P	O	S	A	L	E	Z	V	C	L	L
T	A	U	N	F	O	R	T	U	N	A	T	E	L	Y
O	X	Q	R	E	Q	U	E	S	T	I	O	N	E	S
P	E	X	P	E	C	T	A	T	I	O	N	C	E	W

page 35–36

10 1 nothing/not a lot
2 shipping time
3 15 working days
4 three shifts
5 storage
6 three containers
7 save time and money
8 run more smoothly
9 production planning

page 37

13 1 d 2 g 3 b 4 f 5 c 6 a 7 e

1 · If I win the lottery, (then) I can stop working.
· I can stop working if I win the lottery.
2 · If we get all our work done, (then) we can go home early.
· We can go home early if we get all our work done.
3 · If we get the order, (then) we'll have to work three shifts a day.
· We'll have to work three shifts a day if we get the order.
4 · If I go to the meeting in London, (then) I can also visit the trade fair.
· I can also visit the trade fair if I go to the meeting in London.
5 · If I do the research, (then) I will have to work all weekend.
· I will have to work all weekend if I do the research.
6 · If I attend a PowerPoint course, (then) I can prepare the presentations myself.
· I can prepare the presentations myself if I attend a PowerPoint course.
7 · If we all go together, (then) we can save a lot of money.
· We can save a lot of money if we all go together.

page 38

14 See transcript on page 83.

page 39

15 Possible answers:
1. Is it possible to finish production tomorrow? – It could well be that we will finish production tomorrow.
2. How about building a new production hall? – Unfortunately that cannot be done!
3. Can we have this fabric in pink? – It is impossible to dye this fabric pink.
4. I have to speak to the boss about this now! – I am sorry but it is unlikely he is going to answer his phone at the moment.
5. Can you check stock levels for a blue notebook? – There is a possibility they are sold out already.
6. Are you proposing to double delivery quantity? – It may be the only way to solve the problem.

UNIT 5

page 41

1
1. We are talking about
2. I strongly believe
3. There is a simple explanation
4. What do you mean
5. if I understand

page 42

2 Clarifying information
What do you mean by … ?
If I understand you correctly … ?

Expressing opinions
We are talking about …
I strongly believe that …

3
1. a bonus
2. additional perks

Possible answers:
- What do you mean by additional benefits?
- If I understand you correctly, you are saying that an additional perk is an alternative?
- I strongly believe that additional fringe benefits are an option!
- I imagine we are talking about a different kind of bonus here.

page 42–43

4
1. C Buying a new car? <u>In my opinion</u>, a new engine is still cheaper than a new car!
2. A Round? That is expensive, but <u>I imagine it's something like</u> a square one, only cheaper.
3. B Not enough information? <u>Does that mean</u> I have to give a more detailed explanation?
4. A I understand you think it's expensive! <u>Another option would be</u> to make it smaller.
5. C It can't be fixed? <u>If I understand you correctly</u>, you are telling me that I need a new computer.
6. B Oh dear, <u>we are talking about</u> completely rewriting the documentation for the course.
7. B More feedback? <u>Do you think we can</u> split the work between three people instead?
8. A Something cheaper? <u>Are you suggesting</u> looking for a different type of material?
9. C <u>If you could help me with</u> this matter, <u>I could</u> sort the cheque out straight away.

page 43

5
1. <u>Are you proposing</u> to help out at the meeting?
2. <u>We believe</u> the goods are faulty.
3. <u>Does that mean</u> we have to move to Nottingham?
4. <u>Do you mean</u> you will check on the details?
5. <u>We strongly believe</u> we can work this out.
6. <u>We are talking</u> about an increase of 10%.

page 44

6
1. suggest
2. present
3. payment
4. Company
5. holiday
6. Breakfast

page 45

7 Possible answers:
1. Could the problem be solved by an additional payment of 3.5% into a pension scheme?
2. I think we should look at the private use of the company car.
3. I could imagine an additional three days' paid holiday.
4. I was thinking that a company-paid language course could be an alternative.
5. It might be a possibility to look at vouchers for breakfast and lunch in the canteen.
6. It would be an option to use the fitness and child care facilities for free or, alternatively, have them subsidized.

page 46

8 Possible answers:
1. An additional monthly payment of 3.5% into a pension scheme.
2. Company car can be used privately.

9
1. We were able to work things out.
2. Let us get down to business.
3. It would certainly be an alternative to …
4. So far we have established three alternatives …
5. We have two possibilities but could you imagine …
6. In my opinion that sounds like an option.

1 f 2 a 3 c 4 e 5 d 6 b

page 47

10 1 F 2 F 3 T 4 T 5 F 6 F

11 Possible answers:
1. - Our suggestion is to return the excess amount delivered.
   - It might be a possibility to keep the excess amount and get a discount of 25%.
2. - It would be an option to keep the car and get three inspections free of charge?
   - I think we should take into consideration waiting six weeks until a black car can be delivered.
3. - From my experience the best way is to make an identical new dress/suit.
   - Another option would be to repair the damage at no cost.
4. - We can offer you a pay raise of 3%.
   - It would be an alternative to look at a pay raise of 1.5% and the use of a company car.
5. - We were thinking about a new computer.
   - Do you think we could look at the option to find the fault and repair it?
6. - Do you think we could reduce the price by 7.5%?
   - We could imagine reducing the price if you order larger quantities.

page 48

12

	Synonyms	
offer	quotation	proposal
1 to propose	to suggest	to recommend
2 to increase	to raise	to go up
3 to predict	to forecast	to project
4 to establish	to identify	to determine
5 opinion	belief	position
6 to research	to investigate	to look up
7 objective	aim	goal
8 to solve	to resolve	to tackle

13 1 quotation/proposal
2 resolve/tackle
3 risen/gone up
4 identified/determined
5 suggest/recommend
6 aim/goal
7 to investigate/to look up
8 forecast/project
9 belief/position

UNIT 6

page 50

Starter

agreement	deadlock	disagreement
win–win situation	stalemate	confrontation
deal	impasse	attacks
solutions	standstill	escalation
'golden' bridge		arguments

page 50–51

1 1 T 2 F 3 T 4 T 5 T 6 F

page 51

2 · That is totally unacceptable.
· Could you clarify that, please?
· Let me just make sure I understand what you are saying.
· Where does your information come from?

3 1 c 2 e 3 f 4 b 5 a 6 d

page 52

5 Possible answer:

Dear Simon,

I have just had a most unpleasant conversation with Mr Gilbert in New York about the Student Summer Games. I believe he has some incorrect information from an unnamed 'expert'. His demands ranged from moving the Games to another venue to closing down your factory permanently. He talked about people dying.

However, he did have one point that, if true, would worry me considerably. He claimed the factory would not be closing in August as planned, and due to a new order you would be working overtime through the whole summer.

Therefore, I would like to bring our monthly meeting forward so that we can discuss this telephone call. I can be in your office at 10.30 tomorrow morning. Please let me know if this is convenient.

Best regards
Maurice

6 There are two problems:
Problem: old machines
Bennet's position: – situation better
– factory inspector pleased
– but still need to use old machines
Bayle's position: unhappy, dissatisfied
Measures agreed: none

Problem: new contract
Bennet's position: – must keep to the contract
Bayle's position: – expects the factory to close in the summer
– suggests shift work
Measures agreed: none

page 53

7 1 d 2 e 3 b 4 f 5 a 6 c

8 1 mean   5 position
2 progress   6 complete
3 opinion   7 machines
4 subsidiary   8 shut down

page 54

9 Possible answers:
1 Can you tell me if you can give us a 20% discount?
2 Can you give me an idea of which other British companies you supply?
3 Could you tell me about your company's pollution levels?
4 Can you give me an idea if the pollution is decreasing?
5 Could you tell me about the age of your machinery?
6 Could you tell me how you can prove your company is safe?

page 55–56

10 1 I was horrified, I speak from a position of strength, I have no alternative, I insist
2 I would be very happy to meet, I can quite understand, I am sure that if I were ... , I am very interested ... , what do you feel ... , we need to discuss

page 57

12 Possible solutions:
· The pollution survey finds that the pollution levels are within the EU guidelines.
· Head office suggests that it supply new machines to the factory earlier than planned.
· The work can be done in August and on new, environmentally friendly machines, i.e. not the ones that produce too much pollution.
· The CEO of the chemicals company offers to sponsor all the soft drinks the participants require from the American drinks company.
· The TV producer is replaced by his calmer, more polite boss in the negotiations.

UNIT 7

page 59

1 1 F 2 T 3 F 4 F 5 T

page 60

2 · Fortunately, ...
· I am sure we can find a solution ...

- I have no doubt …
- I had hoped to be able to come to an agreement.
- We are willing to work with that.
- It's a deal!

3 Possible answers:
1. This contract is the result of our mutual agreement.
2. This is certainly a step towards a settlement and a contract.
3. I have no doubt that the seller is open to a last-minute change.
4. Hopefully, we will be able to provide the details in ten days.
5. It seems we still need to discuss the price in order to achieve our objectives.
6. We are very satisfied with the way the talks are going.

page 61

4 Possible answers:
1. We are committed to finding a solution.
2. I can only agree with you there!
3. We are willing to work with that.
4. I have no doubt that will interest him.
5. Fortunately, I was able to talk to my client yesterday.
6. I believe we have made some good progress.

5 1 He will take possession of the houses within eight months.
2. No, he did not. He agreed to a purchase price of 2.5 million.
3. Yes.

page 62

6 1 B   2 C   3 A   4 C   5 B   6 C   7 A

page 63

7 Possible answers:
1. I think we will need a detailed summary of this part of the contract.
2. I can guarantee you that the house is available in July.
3. This is where we stand at the moment.
4. We have covered a lot of ground today!
5. Let's draft the contract based on these points.
6. Let me just repeat these points, if I may.

page 63–64

8
1. drawn up
2. look at the changes
3. signature
4. contract signifies
5. finalized
6. implement
7. guarantee
8. you can go
9. for having us

page 64

9 Possible answers:

Expressing deadlines	Closing discussions
· implement this by … · You will be hearing from us by …	· … thank you for having us. · Well, it has been a pleasure. · Have a nice day!

page 65

10 Possible answers:
- The closing date for submission of the plans is the 9th of August.
- We have to finish the drawings by Monday.
- You will be hearing from us by 4.30 p.m./the 21st/Friday.
- We should come to a decision within the next two weeks/four days in order to solve the problem.
- We have to set a time limit of three weeks to obtain the information.
- There is a deadline of four days/five months to finalize the agreement.
- I would be grateful if you could implement this by the 21st of the month to complete the paperwork.

11 Possible answers:

Scenario 1
Speaker 1
- Thank you for a productive meeting.
- I am/We are very much looking forward to a successful business relationship.
- Thank you for having us.
- We had expected to get a lot out of this meeting, and we did.

Speaker 2
- I/We feel exactly the same!
- So am I/are we, and thank you for coming.
- My/Our pleasure!
- Good to hear. Would you like … ?

Scenario 2
Speaker 1
- Thank you for a fruitful discussion and the customer suggestions that solved the problem.
- I/We would certainly like to intensify my/our business relations with your company.
- If there is nothing else, then we can go and have a look round the factory.
- OK, follow me, please!

Speaker 2
- Don't mention it. One of our priorities is to ensure customer satisfaction.
- That would also be in our interest. It has been a pleasure so far.
- That would be wonderful.

page 66

12
1. We assume
2. please do not hesitate to
3. As discussed
4. please feel free to
5. As you will see
6. look forward
7. Please note
8. Attached

page 68–69

Test yourself!

Across
3. stalemate
5. confrontation
6. minutes
8. reservation
11. agenda
12. venue
15. deadlock
19. schedule
20. opinion
22. pension
23. win-win
25. neutral
26. demand
27. initial offer
28. negotiation

Down
1. objective
2. subsidiaries
4. alternative
6. mutual agreement
7. seller
9. notify
10. tradable
13. deadline
14. proposal
16. option
17. deal
18. counterproposal
21. contract
24. item

Transcripts

UNIT 1, EXERCISE 5

Tasha Hi Karin, please come in!
Karin Hi. What did you want to talk to me about? I imagine it's Jackson's.
Tasha Yes, as you know, we have to talk about the meeting we've planned with them. Have you got the price calculations I asked for?
Karin Yes, and I also brought the quote so we can check the details.
Tasha Great, that's exactly what I need. We'll have to set a target price and a maximum price in order to give us some room to negotiate.
Karin Hmm! … The price shown in the quote isn't too bad. But did you take a look at the delivery and payment terms?
Tasha Yes, I did. Not quite what we expected. We usually get better conditions and payment terms as well as a discount on large quantities.
Karin Yes, in fact, all our other suppliers have improved their discounts to us this year.
Tasha What are our preferred delivery and payment terms?
Karin Sorry, but I'll have to look at the figures again. You'll have them in a day or two. As for the payment terms, I would prefer to talk to Accounts first, if that's OK with you.
Tasha OK, let me know when you have all the details.
Karin No problem.
Tasha You know, we had such a good relationship with our old Chinese suppliers.
Karin Yes, they were always polite and delivered on time until they were taken over by that new company.
Tasha Yes, I know. Well, I hope we manage to work well with the new people.
Karin By the way, have we set a date for our internal meeting yet?
Tasha Adrian and Mirja have both agreed on the 24th of June. Adrian needs a little more time to check the delivery times. Mirja will join us to give us more information about Jackson's since she did the research on them before we contacted them. She thinks that they really need more customers for their new business line.
Karin OK, the 24th sounds good to me. What about Frank?
Tasha Frank is waiting for the final quality report. But he expects it on the 22nd.
Karin OK fine. Anything else?
Tasha Oh, I'll chair the meeting with their sales team. But I need someone to take the minutes of the meeting and an additional person as backup on that day. Could you check when you are available? If you let me know by the 18th, we can set a date to meet them then.
Karin No problem. By the way, did you hear about … ?

UNIT 1, EXERCISE 8

Tasha Frank, I don't believe you have met Mirja, have you? Mirja is our new company secretary. Mirja, Frank is our quality control expert. He works in the research department.
Frank and Mirja Nice to meet you.
Tasha Oh, and this is Karin. She's my assistant. OK, so we are all here. Now let's check that we have all the information we need. Frank?
Mirja Actually, Tasha, I have an appointment with the auditors in 20 minutes. Is it OK with you if I start?
Tasha OK, well, I suppose so. What can you tell us about Jackson's?
Mirja Well, they're an old, established company. They were founded in 1905 and have always had a great reputation for good quality. They have even won a prize at the main trade fair every year for the last ten years.
Frank I heard they're a bit old-fashioned.
Mirja Yes Frank, they are a family company, which is unusual today, and the current CEO is the grandson of the founder. He is only 35 years old, studied engineering and even has a doctorate. That's probably why the whole company is based around their Research and Development division. In fact, that is their strength and they comply with all the latest engineering standards.
Tasha What about their finances?
Mirja Well, as far as I can see, they are completely up to date and have filed all their accounts up to now. Unfortunately, though, they have not been making much profit over the last three years and they had to let some of their key workers go because of fewer customers and orders. Therefore, I think price will be an important issue for them, as well as payment terms. This could also be why they are interested in developing in China.
Tasha Interesting!
Mirja Currently their volume of exports is small, since most of their customers are near their offices. However, there was recently an article by their new sales director, David Hallam, in one of the trade newspapers. He said he was very keen on developing their presence in the Asian market.
Frank I heard they were having financial problems. Tasha, are you sure you want to do business with them?
Tasha Hmm! That really depends on your quality report and anything else Mirja has to say.
Mirja The article says they took part in a delegation that went to China. Jackson's, it seems, have set up a joint venture with a local partner. We would be mostly dealing with the Chinese branch of the business, I think, and they have a good reputation. In fact, according to the article, the company has received a lot of large

orders for the coming year. Of course, we'll have to be sure that they can deliver on time. However, I think we should try to do business with them. ... Oh, Tasha, I'm really sorry, but I must go now. You'll have a copy of my report on your desk tomorrow morning.

Tasha Thanks, Mirja. Now Frank, about the quality report ...

UNIT 2, EXERCISE 6

Harold Hello, Harold Gosling speaking.
DaVita Hello, Harold. Have you sent me the agenda? I can't open my emails, so could you please read the points out to me?
Harold Of course. I've left the venue open as you wanted and used the 18th of February as the date, and included Johannes as a participant.
DaVita Perfect!
Harold Now the bullet points. Firstly, the usual apologies, then corporate centre ...
DaVita No, I want the appointment of the public relations consultant to come next.
Harold OK, secondly, the appointment of public relations consultant, then corporate centres ...
DaVita No, Harold, you've forgotten that the marketing department should be near the top.
Harold OK, thirdly, marketing department. Can I put corporate centres next?
DaVita No, no, not yet, I want notification of customers next, and then corporate centres. Let's get all our important points at the top.
Harold After corporate centres, I've put branch closures, then advertising and corporate image, and branding.
DaVita Yes, and finally?
Harold Well, I have call centres, then computers, and finally AOB.
DaVita It would be better to swap the call centres and the computers around. Then it's fine.
Harold Do you want to check the agenda again?
DaVita No, just send it off as soon as it's finished. Geoff can sign it.

UNIT 2, EXERCISE 8

Mary Hello, Oracle Bank, Mary Jellico speaking. How can I help you?
Shirley Hello, Ms Jellico. Shirley Smithson from Dominions Bank here. How are you?
Mary I'm fine thanks, and you?
Shirley Fine. I'm calling to arrange the meeting and discuss the agenda.
Mary Do you have any more points?
Shirley Yes, I do. Have you received the agenda?
Mary Yes, I have. We suggested the 11th of February, at 9.00 a.m.
Shirley The time is acceptable. But we can't make the 11th as Mrs DaVita will be away until the 16th. How about the 18th of February, at 9.00 a.m.? Is that OK?
Mary I think that will be fine. I will confirm that later, though. Any other points?
Shirley No, but can we move public relations up the agenda?
Mary Yes, that should be fine. I will move it to after the apologies for absence. OK?
Shirley Fine. However, some other things also need moving as they go together with the public relations issue. For example, customer notification, branding and advertising.
Mary OK. And is adding the company car issue OK with you?
Shirley Yes, OK, and all the points on computers can be combined. They are lower priority. But redundancy payments should come after the closure of the corporate centres.
Mary No problem. So we have agreed on the date, the 18th of February, and the time, 9.00 a.m., in our boardroom here at Oracle. I'll check and confirm the date and time of the meeting in writing. So could you redo the agenda as discussed and email it to me?
Shirley Of course, I'll do it as soon as possible.

UNIT 3, EXERCISE 4

Joanna Joanna Duncan, Books to Go. How can I help you?
Mark Hello, Joanna, Mark Taylor from Bookmark here. How are you?
Joanna I'm fine, thanks. And you?
Mark Very well, thanks. Have you received the revised agenda, Joanna?
Joanna Yes, I have. It was in my inbox this morning.
Mark Great! Shall we go ahead on this basis?
Joanna Actually, our sales director has reminded us that we need to discuss pricing policy as well, because ...
Mark Yes, right. Of course, we'll need to speak about that as well. But can we discuss that at a later meeting?
Joanna Well, it will affect the advertising. You see, this point is important to us because we often need to cut prices dramatically to promote sales.
Mark Oh yes, I see. How about putting pricing, then, before advertising?
Joanna Oh, OK, thanks, Mark. That's a good idea.
Mark And what about the other arrangements?
Joanna Everything else is fine, Mark. So I look forward to meeting you in London.
Mark Same here, Joanna. See you on the 13th. Goodbye.
Joanna Bye.

UNIT 3, EXERCISE 9

Narrator The meeting at Bookmark's
Rachel Brian, this meeting is vital to us. If we can get a quick agreement, it will help with sales. They're at an all-time low this month, and that makes it hard to pay the bills.
Brian Yes, Rachel, our customer base is starting to cause big problems. If we don't get some new and especially younger customers, we'll have many more problems in the future. If we had thought of this earlier, we would have already been able to improve sales. So if we increase the range of stock available, that should help. However, I would prefer to only take on their better quality titles.
Mark To be honest, I think BTG have problems, too. But after this first meeting I think we will be in a better position to make decisions. OK, so

		let's work on our goals for the meeting first.
	Rachel	Fine. So we want them to help organize a joint website.
	Brian	Yes, and if they do that and contribute to the costs, will we also have access to their catalogue of self-help and business development books?
	Mark	Yes, we will. But we should make that our offer in exchange and not let them see that it's something we need. We'll just say – if they work with us on the website, we'll let them sell their books in our stores.
	Brian	Oh, I get it. That is a plus for them. But actually, it is our main target.
	Mark	(Laughs) That's the idea!
	Narrator	The meeting at Books to Go
	Valentine	Is the website ready yet?
	George	Not yet, Val. I haven't paid the last invoice. So the designer has stopped work on it.
	Valentine	What's the idea here, George? The website is vital for our future. And we have the money.
	George	Look, Val, I want to wait until after the meeting. We might get some money out of Bookmark's. However, if we say we have already covered all the costs, they might not want to contribute.
	Valentine	Right, George, I understand. So, we have to pretend that the website is still an idea, not already designed.
	George	That's it, and anyway, adding their content will slow the designer down. I'll take our original designs to show them. That should do it.
	Paul	OK, but we must get our books into their market. I know their standards are very high, but English language books are selling well in Europe at the moment, especially self-help and language learning titles.
	Valentine	Agreed, Paul. I'll hold out for a good deal on our list of non-fiction. If they give us that, I won't insist on including fiction as well. Or perhaps only the women's titles? That list is huge.
	Paul	Great idea, Val!

UNIT 3, EXERCISE 11

	Joseph	Hello, Mr Stevens, it's very nice to see you again. May I introduce you to my colleague Brian Newson? He's our Operations Director.
	Valentine	How do you do, Mr Newson? Very pleased to meet you. I don't think you have met Dennis Griffith. Dennis is our website expert. He has been advising us on developing our online presence.
	Joseph and Dennis	How do you do?
	Joseph	It is a pleasure to meet you. How long have you been in the Internet field?
	Dennis	For about ten years now. I used to work for Mega-Online in New York. By the way, please call me Dennis.
	Joseph	Thanks, you can call me Joseph. Ah, I think we should take our seats now. It's time to begin. Ladies and gentlemen, please take your seats around the table. We'll …

UNIT 4, EXERCISE 1

	Richard	Excuse me, everyone. Can I ask you to come back to our agenda, please? OK. Let's focus on the next item on the agenda, which is the delivery time and terms. Jason, over to you.
	Jason	Thank you, Richard. Marcy, the initial offer states an average production time of 15 working days for the material. This seems to be a bit long, since we also have to add four working days for transportation. Would it be possible to deliver in ten working days plus transportation time?
	Marcy	Hmm! … The lengthy delivery time is due to the quantity you are looking at. We require two working days to set up the production line, at least ten working days for the production run, one day for the agreed quality checks, and one day for loading.
	Jason	Well, then, is a shorter production time feasible at all?
	Marcy	Jason, I assume you are referring to our shift system. Well, we are currently working a two-shift day and could possibly extend to a third shift. But that would result in a price increase due to additional staff costs. It would take about six days off the delivery time, though.
	Jason	Hmm … Richard, what's your opinion?
	Richard	For the time being, let's make a note of it. However, are there any alternatives?
	Marcy	An alternative would be partial-shipments at seven-day intervals.
	Jason	Sorry, Marcy, but on an ex works basis that would increase the delivery costs dramatically.
	Georgina	May I interrupt?
	Jason	Sure!
	Georgina	Marcy, can I have a word with you, please?
	Marcy	Is it OK with you if we take a short break?
	Richard	Of course. Is five minutes enough?
	Marcy	Yes, more than enough!
		…
	Marcy	Thank you for your patience. Tell me … How much material can be stored here at your warehouse?
	Craig	We have storage capacity for two full container loads in our warehouse at the moment. Why do you want to know?
	Marcy	Well, if it were possible to also store a third, then we could deliver the overall amount in three shipments of three containers instead of four shipments of two containers spread out over the year. The added benefit is that it would save time and, due to the increased overall amount, also money.
	Jason	Well, Marcy, you certainly have given Craig and me something to think about. Richard, maybe we can discuss this over lunch. Hmm?
	Richard	Marcy, shall we break for lunch now?
	Marcy	That's fine with me. How about the rest?
	Richard	OK, listen up. Shall we meet back here at 2 p.m. to continue as we …

UNIT 4, EXERCISE 7

Jason ... That's right. This morning we talked about (1) earlier delivery, part-shipment, an additional shift, and increased order quantities. We have looked at each alternative very carefully. We are unable to accept (2) a third shift.

Marcy Well, I guessed you wouldn't want that because of the increase in price. However, it is a solution if there is a major increase in demand which needs to be met quickly.

Jason At the moment, that's not going (3) to happen. But who knows?

Marcy There is also the possibility of shipping the goods at intervals. What do you think of that?

Jason Unfortunately, that is not an option (4) either, because once again we would be looking at a price increase. Transport is really getting more and more costly these days!

Marcy True, but that depends, then, on which forwarder you use. Maybe (5) I would be able to help you negotiate a very good price with our forwarder. Would you like me to try? I'm sure he'll be interested in dealing with you.

Jason Of course! If you think that you can do (6) that. But we would have to look at that again at a later date, though.

Marcy OK, I've made a note of it and we'll let you know.

Jason Thank you, Marcy. Good. Now, Craig wants to discuss the final proposal with you. Craig?

Craig Your question was about storage capacity. Maybe we can (7) do it. We've checked and with a little careful planning we could store three containers.

Marcy Good to hear. However, I have another suggestion. There is also the possibility of adjusting order quantities according to your needs. Let's say, three containers in one shipment as discussed, two in another, or even four, if necessary. This would be OK as long as we stick to the overall order quantities we agreed to.

Craig That is a nice offer. But we can't (8) store four containers, unless we build another warehouse, and that means no (9). Still ... ordering two containers is an alternative, should there be any changes.

UNIT 4, EXERCISE 14

Richard Can we reduce transportation time by sea freight from six to four weeks?

Richard Is there a possibility to reduce transportation time by sea freight from six to four weeks?

Marcy It is impossible to reduce the transportation time, because of the shipping routes used.

Richard Do you think we can have a further discount of 2.5%?

Richard Is it conceivable that we could have a further discount of 2.5%?

Marcy Unfortunately, that cannot be done because of the price for raw materials at the moment.

Richard Is the price increasing on the commodities market?

Richard Is it possible that the price will increase on the commodities market?

Marcy It could be that the price will increase this year.

Richard Will there be a shortage of container space on ships in the near future?

Richard Do you think that there will be a shortage of container space on ships in the near future?

Marcy I consider it to be a possibility because the volume of exports is rising.

Richard Is the exchange rate staying at its current level?

Richard Can it be expected that the exchange rate will stay at its current level?

Marcy It is hardly likely to stay at its current level, due to the continued decline of the dollar.

Richard Are you opening another production plant?

Richard Could it well be that you are opening another production plant?

Marcy We can rule out the possibility of opening another production plant, because there are no suitable properties available.

UNIT 5, EXERCISE 1

Yamamoto ... Yes, this is very encouraging and I am looking forward to seeing the figures for the third and fourth quarter. Now ... let's talk about you, Dwight. You have been with us for a long time.

Dwight Yes, for over 15 years. And I have enjoyed every minute of it. It is certainly a challenging, but satisfying job.

Yamamoto I am very glad to hear it. Well, I have read the proposal you forwarded me and have to say, though, that a pay increase of 10% is out of the question. You know you are already at the top of the pay scale.

Dwight To be honest, Mr Yamamoto, that is really rather disappointing. You know, we are talking about my first pay raise in more than four years. I have managed to acquire a lot of new customers and increase order volume with existing customers. Surely that deserves recognition, doesn't it?

Yamamoto Dwight, I strongly believe that we can come to an agreement. Unfortunately, though, I just cannot agree to 10%! I can defend an increase of 4% to the members of the board. But that is really as far as I am willing to go.

Dwight 4%? That's not a great deal, is it?

Yamamoto Dwight, there is a simple explanation for this. If you remember, none of the staff have had a pay raise in the last four years because business has been very difficult. Bonus payments were also suspended. And, as you know, last year we awarded a pay raise of 2.5% to our workforce. This year, we will finally be able to re-activate the bonus system. So, you see, if we agree on 4% you will receive a higher pay raise than everyone else.

Dwight Hmm, what do you mean by a higher pay raise? The next staff pay raise is due in August, and if they negotiate 1.5% for the next twelve months, I will only break even and not have gained anything.

Yamamoto Well, I did mention that we are going to re-activate the bonus system. That would certainly be an increase in pay.

Dwight	So, if I understand you correctly, you are telling me that I can take it or leave it?	Yamamoto	It can, indeed! Does that mean you have looked at that possibility as well?
Yamamoto	Dwight, I am sorry. But 4% is the best I can do!	Dwight	Now that … would be giving away my secrets, wouldn't it?
Dwight	Mr Yamamoto, if we can't agree on more than 4%, how about looking at additional perks?	Yamamoto	Hmm, I know what you mean!
Yamamoto	Yes, that would be an alternative … OK, OK! I feel we should continue this conversation once you have come up with some options. Send me your proposals and we will talk again. I am confident we can work this out.	Dwight	Mr Yamamoto, so far we have established three alternatives, which both of us seem to be quite happy with in comparison with my original proposal, which you rejected. I think it's time we settled for one, don't you?
Dwight	OK, fine. Thank you, Mr Yamamoto. Bye now.	Yamamoto	Well, yes, I do. Dwight, all of these options have advantages for both you and Nacatomi. We favour the language courses because of the benefits to daily business. That they are tax-deductible is an added bonus. In addition, the course will also help to secure your position as head of international sales and boost your ability to deal directly with our French and Spanish partners.
Yamamoto	Goodbye.		
Dwight	Hmm, this is awkward!		

UNIT 5, EXERCISE 9

a Let's get down to business …
b In my opinion that sounds like an option.
c It would certainly be an alternative to …
d We have two possibilities, but could you imagine …
e So far we have established three alternatives …
f We were able to work things out.

UNIT 5, EXERCISE 10

Dwight	Ah, good morning, Mr Yamamoto. How are you?
Yamamoto	Fine, thanks. How are you, Dwight?
Dwight	Very well, but very busy.
Yamamoto	You always are, Dwight, you always are! Let's get down to business, then. I have considered your proposals. Would you like to give me some more details?
Dwight	Of course. I could well imagine that the additional monthly payment into the pension scheme is beneficial to Nacatomi, because the payments are fully tax-deductible.
Yamamoto	Yes, in my opinion that sounds like an option. It would increase your pension when you retire. How about the private use of a company car? I cannot see the advantage there.
Dwight	The company pays insurance, tax, fuel, and maintenance on the company cars, and it doesn't matter if the cars are used or not. I would pay the tax and social security contributions on the mileage driven, through my salary.
Yamamoto	Does that mean you would have to record your trips in a log book?
Dwight	Yes, it does. What do you think?
Yamamoto	Let me see. It would certainly be an alternative to your initial proposal of a 10% pay raise. I admit that this would be helpful.
Dwight	I am glad to hear that!
Yamamoto	Dwight, you have obviously researched the proposals in detail and I can see the advantages to both you and Nacatomi Corporation. We have two possibilities, but could you imagine a third one, such as an intensive language course financed by the company? As head of international sales, it would be a good idea to brush up on your Spanish and French. That would certainly help you in daily business. Wouldn't you agree?
Dwight	Yes, I would have to agree. The course can be set off against taxes, can't it?

Dwight	OK, that's settled, then. 4% and a company-financed language course. I am really quite pleased that we were able to work things out, Mr Yamamoto.
Yamamoto	So am I, Dwight! I'll get my secretary to forward the details to you as soon as possible. Just sign the form and return it by fax. You can start having a look for suitable language schools now.
Dwight	OK. Thank you.
Yamamoto	My pleasure. Bye, then.
Dwight	Goodbye.

UNIT 6, EXERCISE 1

Gilbert	Gilbert here. Is that Maurice Bayle?
Bayle	Yes, Bayle here.
Gilbert	This situation is totally unacceptable. It is a pollution disaster.
Bayle	I am sorry, Mr Gilbert. Could you clarify that, please? Pollution disaster? The pollution is at acceptable levels.
Gilbert	Acceptable? How can you say that?
Bayle	Let me make sure I understand what you are saying! Do you mean that the factory is doing something against the law?
Gilbert	Yes! No country allows such a high level of pollution. You don't have a clue. Our experts say that people die from these chemicals every year. You know we are the ones who are paying for these Games. But we will not release the money yet. We call the shots here.
Bayle	But, Mr Gilbert, I can assure you that the pollution level has been going down for the past three years. Where did you get your information from?
Gilbert	Huh! I'll go over your head. Let me speak to your superiors! I have friends in high places.
Bayle	Mr Gilbert, I am the mayor, and my superiors are the townspeople. How can we solve this problem together?
Gilbert	Do you really think we can bring 2,000 young athletes to your polluted town? The Games must definitely be moved. You're just not in the loop! Didn't you know the factory has a large, new order for dangerous ant poison? It seems it'll be working overtime all through the summer.

Bayle	I am afraid we cannot move the Games. Have you spoken to Mr Bennet about this? After all, he is your co-sponsor and he has agreed to cover half the costs. Oh, and please ask your expert to contact me and I will explain everything to him. In the meantime, I'll try and find out about this new order. Hmm, how strange! The factory usually closes for two to three weeks in August.
Gilbert	To tell you the truth, I'm not interested in your excuses. We have to make sure the Games are safe. If not, the whole thing will be a non-starter. Please understand we cannot take any risks!
Bayle	Mr Gilbert, let's not forget two important things here! The Games have already been organized and the company employs 50% of our population. Therefore, the Games can definitely not be moved.
Gilbert	Ridiculous! It must be possible to do something. I'll get back to you. The man just doesn't get the message!
Bayle	Goodbye, Mr Gilbert.

UNIT 6, EXERCISE 6

Bennet	Hello, Maurice.
Bayle	Bonjour, Simon. I am so pleased you could see me at such short notice.
Bennet	No problem at all, and I'm sorry to hear about your difficult conversation with Mr Gilbert. Come and sit down. Let's discuss the matter!
Bayle	Mr Gilbert was rather rude. I am happy I didn't lose my temper. How's the factory? Mr Gilbert mentioned a new contract.
Bennet	Fine. The factory's inspector thinks we have been making good progress with the new machines. Nevertheless, some of the old machines are still dirty, and we will unfortunately still need to use them in the summer. Our goal is, however, to produce the amount in the contract by the end of August in order to allow time for shipping.
Bayle	And does this mean the company will not shut down during the Student Summer Games?
Bennet	Unfortunately, yes. I am not in a position to shut the factory down, because we must achieve our targets. It is, in fact, company policy to close loss-making subsidiaries.
Bayle	But the company is profitable, isn't it?
Bennet	Well, we have been losing money for the last three years – this can't continue. What do you suggest I do?
Bayle	Hmm, I'm not sure. But from my experience, the best way is to set up flexible working schedules which allow day and night shifts. Or, better still, change the delivery schedule for the goods to a later date.
Bennet	Unfortunately, I'm not in a position to change it, because head office has signed the contract.
Bayle	Oh, I appreciate your position. But can you offer any alternatives?
Bennet	To be honest, I am not really certain now. You know we need this order to keep people employed.
Bayle	Yes, I completely understand what you're saying. But as far as the TV company is concerned, they will not sponsor the Games if we cannot reduce the pollution. Can you offer any alternatives? How important is it for you that the work is done in Dyersville?
Bennet	Well, we have no alternative, Maurice. The work must be done here. Moving it is not an option. This is a head office directive.
Bayle	And Simon, you would use the old machines, too. I must say I am very dissatisfied with that solution. However, I understand your position. Well, I need to get back to my office and give the whole thing some thought. Perhaps you could contact your head office again and explain to them the situation with the American TV company.

UNIT 6, EXERCISE 12

Bayle	We really have to solve this matter now. They all want to make their points.
Bennet	I agree, and I think we should let them. However, I think our head office have come up with a good solution. They have found a way to build a 'golden' bridge. It will mean spending some money, but …
Bayle	That is excellent. Tell me more!
Bennet	Oh, later, Maurice, later! It's not confirmed yet. We are also arranging for a pollution survey. So please see that people co-operate with the testers.
Bayle	What do you mean?
Bennet	Well, the university will be sending some students to take measurements and samples, and you'll have a full report by Friday. I will give everyone more details at the meeting.
Bayle	That's great. But, Simon, what if the report is bad?
Bennet	Maurice, let's not worry about that now. Set your meeting for Friday, and I'll be there.

UNIT 7, EXERCISE 1

Clark	Nice to see you again, Mr Fisher. I hope all is well?
Fisher	Yes, thank you for asking.
Clark	Fortunately, I was able to speak to my client yesterday and he is happy with the agreement so far. Is there anything that we still need to discuss?
Fisher	Well … there is. Afterwards I spoke to my partners and we came to the conclusion that we really don't want to include fitted kitchens and garden sheds in the entire project, after all. If about half of the houses have them, that's enough. We think it's just money we don't need to spend.
Clark	Oh, I am sure we can find a solution here. I have no doubt that my client will be open to considering this last-minute change. Let me just call him!
	…
	Yes, thank you so much. My pleasure! I will call you back later then. Bye.

86 | Transcripts

I had hoped to be able to come to an agreement with my client and, fortunately, I have. If we sign the contract today, he is willing to add in the price of the kitchens and the garden sheds in the purchase price. It is an extremely good offer. Would you like to discuss it with your partners first?

Fisher Yes, just give me a moment. I need to send them a text message because they are in a meeting themselves. ... Done!
Clark Would you like some coffee?
Fisher Yes please! It's unfortunate that my partners are unable to be here today. But ... oh, that was quick. Here is the answer. Well, we are willing to work with that.
Clark Excellent. I am very pleased.
Fisher It's a deal then!
Clark OK. So, let's have coffee, and then ...

UNIT 7, EXERCISE 5
19

The discussion continues:
Clark Right, now let's get back to business and bring this negotiation to a head!
Fisher Yes, let's. I must say, all in all, we have covered a lot of ground in the past two weeks, haven't we?
Clark Yes, we certainly have.
Fisher Well, do you think that we will be able to take possession of the houses within eight months?
Clark Hmm, I can assure you that my client is true to his word and you will be able to start work on the project by the agreed date.
Fisher Brilliant! But can we make a note of that in the contract?
Clark Let's approach this another way, then! So far we have established that for the sum of 2.5 million, the properties in the Holland Drive development include in the purchase price a fitted kitchen and a garden shed per house. In addition, the handover date we've agreed to is the 1st of June. Finally, the contract is to be drawn up today and signed by both parties early this evening. This should cover all the details.
Fisher Just to make sure, let me repeat, if I may!
Clark Sure!
Fisher 2.5 million, kitchens and garden sheds included and the date of handover is the 1st of June, right?
Clark Yes, absolutely right. Let's draft the contract based on these points for signature later today. I suggest we meet again at around 4.30 p.m. to continue. Does that suit you?
Fisher Yes, it does. I'll see you in a couple of hours, then.
Clark Great, I'll have all the papers ready and then we can ...

UNIT 7, EXERCISE 8
20

Clark Thank you for your patience today, Mr Fisher. I really appreciate it.
Fisher No problem, Mr Clark. We both know that this was necessary. Have you drawn up the contract?
Clark Yes, would you like to go through it once more?
Fisher No, not really. I only want to look at the changes we've discussed today and then I will sign the document. Oh, has your client signed it already?
Clark Yes, and if you turn to the last page, his signature is right ... there.
Fisher Hmm, oh, yes. Thank you. OK, give me a moment, please! Right, yes, I'm happy with that.
Clark Congratulations, Mr Fisher! This contract signifies the successful conclusion of a lot of hard work over the past couple of weeks.
Fisher Well, it does, doesn't it? My partners and I are very pleased, as well. So, what happens now?
Clark When we have finalized the contract, we will submit it to the relevant authorities.
Fisher Hmm, I know this may sound a bit impatient, but we would be grateful if you could implement this by the end of the week.
Clark Mr Fisher, I guarantee you that you will be hearing from us by Thursday at the very latest. I hope that meets with your approval.
Fisher Of course. Then we can guarantee access to the project site any time we would like, can't we?
Clark Yes, you can. In fact, you can go next Monday. ... Well, it has been a pleasure.
Fisher Yes, it has. I also speak for my partners when I say thank you for having us.
Clark So, what is the plan for this evening, then? Will you ... ?

Useful phrases

PROVIDING REASONS AND EXPLANATIONS

This is because … .
The reason for … is … .
… is essential for our customers.
These are the most important points … .
We must have … .
We have to have … .

We need/require … .
We want … .
We would like … .
This is a must!
The price must fit our guideline.
Money is all-important!

EXPRESSING HIT

Have
We must …
Our main concern is …
It is vital/crucial that …
I refuse to accept …

Intend
Our intention is …
I would like to …
We might like to …

Tradable
I am willing to accept … if …
I think we will have to agree to …
It would be an alternative to …
We can trade this against …
A few things we can compromise on are …

PRESENTING PROPOSALS/COUNTERPROPOSALS

I/We propose/suggest …
How about … ?
Would it be possible … ?
How do you feel about … ?
Would/Could you accept/consider … ?

ASKING FOR AND CLARIFYING INFORMATION

… is correct, isn't it?
Can you tell me how … ?
Is it alright with you if … ?
Would it be possible … ?
It seems … What is your opinion?

EXPRESSING POSSIBILITIES/PROBABILITIES

It is possible/probable/conceivable (that) …
There is a possibility (that) …
It may be …
It could well be that …
In all probability …
It is to be expected …

EXPRESSING IMPOSSIBILITIES/IMPROBABILITIES

It is impossible to …
It is out of the question …
Unfortunately, that cannot be done!
We can rule out the possibility of …
It is doubtful whether/if …
It is (hardly) likely …

CLARIFYING INFORMATION

Do you suggest … ?
Are you suggesting that … ?
Do you mean … ?
Does that mean … ?
If I understand you correctly … ?
What do you mean by … ?

EXPRESSING OPINIONS

In my/our opinion …
From our/my point of view …
We are talking/speaking about …
We are/I am of the opinion that …
We/I strongly believe/feel that …
I am confident that …
I/We imagine it something like …

RESPONDING TO PROPOSALS

There are several options …
That would depend on …
Now that you mention it …
Considering this I/we would …
It sounds like an alternative/option/possibility …

SUGGESTING SOLUTIONS

I/We could imagine …
I/We think we should …
I was/We were thinking that …
It would be helpful/an option …
It might be possible to/a possibility …
From my/our experience, the best way …
Do you think we can/could … ?
Could the problem be solved by … ?

ASKING THE RIGHT QUESTION

Open questions
Why is that so important to you?
Where does your information come from?
Do you have key managers in your company?
What can you offer us?

Indirect questions
Can you give me an idea of your … ?
Could you tell me … ?
How do you think we can achieve this goal?

EXPRESSIONS FOR DISAGREEING

Polite
I would prefer …
That is not how we see it.
Could you clarify that, please?
Could you explain that more fully, please?
I'm afraid we couldn't agree to that.

Less polite
You are wrong.
That is totally unacceptable.
No, that is out of the question.
No, I'm not interested.
I think you should explain.
I don't see the point.
Our experts say that …

Expressions to slow conversation down
Let me (just) make sure I understand what you are saying.
Let's go back and review the situation.
Why is that important to you?
How can we deal with/solve this problem?
Where does your information come from?

EXPRESSIONS FOR DEALING WITH DISAGREEMENT OR DEADLOCK

Making suggestions
Could the problem be solved by … ?
Can you offer any alternatives?

Clarifying
Does that mean … ?
How important is it for you that … ?
What is the purpose of this policy?

Asking for suggestions
Can you offer us any other possibility?
What would you suggest?
What do you suggest I do?

Expressing partial agreement
I understand how you feel!
I agree with you specifically on …
Yes, you have a point there about …

PHRASES TO CALM A SITUATION AND RESOLVE PROBLEMS

Asking questions
Could you tell us why you feel like that?
How can we reach a compromise?
What do you think is a fair way to resolve … ?
Your position is very interesting. Can you tell me more?

Asking for or encouraging agreement with views
Do you agree with our position on … ?
Do you feel you can accept … ?
I hope you can see our point of view.
Let me explain our position!

Expressing agreement
I know exactly what you mean.
I believe that is correct.
That seems reasonable.
If I were in your position, I would also …

MOVING NEGOTIATIONS ALONG

Describing current/future situations
Fortunately, …
Unfortunately, we haven't been able to …
We are very satisfied/dissatisfied …
In future, we hope to …
Hopefully, we will be able to …
By the time we …

Expressing agreement
I/We can only agree with you there.
I/We have to admit that you are right.
I am/We are willing to work with that.
That is also our concern/point of view/goal.
By mutual agreement we have decided to …
It's a deal!

Conveying commitment
I am/We are sure we can find a solution to …
I am/We are committed to finding a solution.
I/We have no doubt that we …
We hope to be able to come to an agreement.
We are looking forward to a successful business relationship.

Stating progress made or current status
I believe we have made some good progress.
This is certainly a step towards …
Fine, but it seems we still need to discuss …
In order to achieve our objectives, we still …

BRINGING NEGOTIATIONS TO A HEAD

Guaranteeing
I/We guarantee you that …
I/We can assure you that …
I/We will do my/our best to …

Discussing follow-up documentation
Shall we put this into a written proposal?
I think we will need a detailed summary of this.
Let's draft a contract based on these points.

Summarizing
(Just) to summarize …
So far we have established …
Let me just repeat, if I may.
This is where we stand.
I would like to summarize as follows …
I/We think/believe we all agree here that …
We have certainly covered a lot of ground today!

BRINGING NEGOTIATIONS TO A CLOSE

Expressing deadlines
We should come to a decision within/by …
You will be hearing from us by …
The closing date for … is …
I/We would be grateful if you could implement this by …

Closing discussion
Thank you for coming.
Thank you for having us.
Thank you for a fruitful discussion/productive meeting.
I/We had hoped/expected to get a lot out of this meeting.
I am/We are very much looking forward to …
We would certainly like to intensify …